Howard Mylett

INTO THE PSYCHE

headpress 17

Illustrated

Panther
586 04390 X

Mikita Brottman
J.R. Bruun
Eugene Carfax
Michael Carlson
John Carter
Giles Clark
Simon Collins
Dogger
Anthony Ferguson
David Greenall
Mark Griffiths
Stewart Home
Martin Jones
Howard Lake
Marne Lucas
James Marriott
Ben Naylor
Mike Noon
Pan Pantziarka
Julie Peasley
Anthony Petkovich
Rik Rawling
Jack Sargeant
David Graham Scott
Phil Tonge
Sarah Turner
Simon Whitechapel
Joe Scott Wilson

Contents

HEADPRESS

into the psyche

ISBN 1 900486 04 0
ISSN 1353-9760

A Catalogue Record for this Book is available from the British Library

Hello viewers. Lots of exciting developments of late: The reaction to the news that Headpress journal would increase its page count as of No 18 has been favourable. Some readers wanted it to stay the same size at the same price (not much chance of that, lads), but the majority who responded wanted more pages without cutting back on the number of editions published per year. (The letter reproduced on the Lettuce Pages is fairly typical of those received.) The result: Bigger Headpress, same number of editions per year (three). That said, the new format won't see publication until January '99, as your humble editor takes time out to concentrate on the Killing for Culture follow-up tome, See No Evil, with David Slater.

Other news: Russ Kick's Psychotropedia: A Guide to Publications on the Periphery is running late due to the fact that the sheer volume of material covered has caused the estimated page count to triple (final page count is 576)! Apologies to those who have already ordered the book. As a mark of good will, we'll be letting the book go to these patient folk at the original cover price. To everyone else the price is now £15.95. Without a doubt, Psychotropedia will prove to be the most comprehensive work of its type and essential reading for anyone with an interest in the arcane. Due out end-August '98.

Still on the subject of books... Anthony Petkovich's The X Factory: Inside the American Hardcore Film Industry has recently been reprinted. The first edition sold out in a month, and already this edition is shifting fast. If you have yet to savour its delights, we suggest you don't hang around for too long — after this printing, who knows when next it might see the light of day.

Now available in a completely updated and revised edition is Sex Murder Art: The Films of Jörg Buttgereit. New photos, new chapters, new info on the controversial director of Nekromantik, who is currently filming an episode of the curious TV sci-fi series Lexx: The Dark Zone Stories in Canada, as we speak.

Further details on all the above are available in the pages which follow. Happy trails.

—David Kerekes

front cover Marisa Carr as Dolly Blue (Photo © Cathy T. / Dragon Ladies)

layout/design David Kerekes & Walt Meaties

proof-reading Simon Whitechapel

acknowledgements Jörg Buttgereit, Marisa Carr, Sophie Cossette, Joseph Coughlin, Creation Books, Maxon Crumb, Sue Curtis (Taschen), Mark Farrelly, Harvey Fenton (FAB Press), Antonio Ghura, Katharine Gifford, Russ Kick, Stefan Jaworzyn, Adrian Jones, Lesley Kerekes, David Lewis (Medusa), Chris Mikul, Amanda Moss, Heidi Reitmaier (ICA), Roger Sabin, H.E. Sawyer, David Slater, Louis Theroux, Claire Thompson (Turnaround), Anna Vallois (Titan Books), Jason Wilcox.

Art © Ben Naylor / Burning Headpress logo: Bill Babouris

EDITORIAL

HARDCORE CRUMB

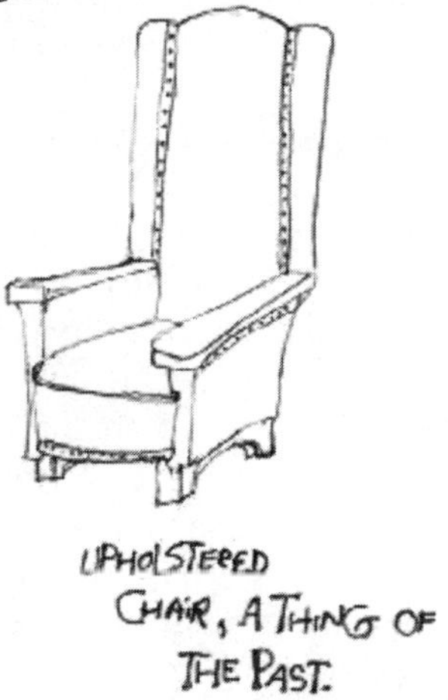

UPHOLSTERED CHAIR, A THING OF THE PAST.

An interview with Maxon Crumb

Anthony Petkovich

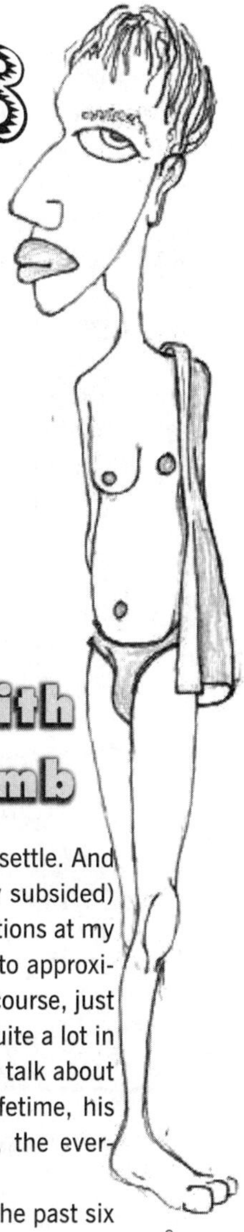

two and a half years after the release of Crumb, I got together with Maxon (the youngest of the brothers documented in Terry Zwigoff's 1995 film) for an interview. A friend, off and on, for about 10 years, Maxon basically felt he had more to say about his life than what was covered in Zwigoff's family portrait. So Maxon patiently awaited for the Crumb "dust" to settle. And by mid-1997 (when the public buzz over video and laser disk sales had safely subsided) he was ready to talk. Our "interview" was really just a bunch of taped conversations at my house, taking place over a period of about a month, and ultimately amounting to approximately 16 hours' worth of gab. A number of these very informal chats were, of course, just pure bullshit — or, rather, bull*shitting*. But Maxon himself admits there's still quite a lot in the conversations which he's never publicly divulged, including highly personal talk about brothers Charles and Robert, Maxon's dabblings with molestation, his past lifetime, his religious beliefs, and many other strange, provocative topics including, yes, the ever-present Crumb.

Maxon and I talked a lot probably because a lot has happened to him over the past six years (i.e., before, during, and after the release of Zwigoff's film) — some of it good, some of it not so good. As stated at the conclusion of Crumb, Charles committed suicide while the film was in post-production. In turn, just after the film's release, Maxon had a *grand mal* seizure, landing him in the hospital for a week, and leaving him in almost continual need of a cane. And — following the superstition that bad things happen in threes — Maxon's mother died in the spring of '97.

But positive things have happened in Maxon's life, as well.

Now in his early 50s, Maxon doesn't really know how to translate the public's sudden interest in his work... let alone comprehend the public itself. But he is grateful for the subsequent projects with which the notoriety from Crumb has helped him secure. Since the movie's release, Maxon has written, edited, and co-illustrated the much-awaited Crumb Family Comix Book — a textual history of his art-obsessed family. He's also successfully selling his surreal paintings on the San Francisco art gallery circuit; has enjoyed some minor acclaim for his bizarre, comical renderings of Edgar Allan Poe stories and poems in Maxon's Poe; is illustrating hard-boiled detective fiction for Genesis magazine; and has written a wonderfully twisted novella entitled Hardcore Mother which no pub-

3

lisher, yet, has had the balls to touch on account of its "politically-incorrect" sexual content.

Despite all of Maxon's recent good — and not so good — fortune, he still leads a very modest, highly disciplined life. Crumb is still alive and well in San Francisco.

headpress **Did you get sexually aroused while writing Hardcore Mother?**

maxon A little, yeah. (Laughs) I think the thing is really sexy. Actually, Robert got kind of professionally righteous about the whole thing, saying that, "Magazines will not take anything that portrays violence towards women." Of course, his violence towards women is more slapstick and gymnastic, but the stuff I wrote about in Hardcore Mother is more about torture… twisted, sick shit — but that's what sex *is* all about. I think it's a good story because it shows that there's no end to sex; the sex-based thing gets into intricate emotional pleasures which naturally develop into sadomasochism. Because, see, in my past lifetime I was this pervert, heavy into sadomasochism. Talk to any holy man and he'll tell you, "Oh yeah, in my past lifetime I was *heavy* into sex." They always hand out that line. Now they're paying for it. Now they have all these restrictions where they can't get away with this, and they can't do that because they've reversed the karma.

Were you trying to resolve something in your own psyche with Hardcore Mother?

No. I was just trying to portray the fact that sex is heavy, and intricate, and convoluted. Take art; no matter how many aeons that people do art, there's always some guy who comes up with a new wrinkle in it, a new way of looking at things, of portraying things, and a whole new inroad gets started. It's the same thing with sex. You just go deeper and deeper and deeper into the emotions involved in sex, the thrills, the pleasures in these great moments and all this shit. Incest is one thing. Lesbianism is another thing. But we don't *know* how deep human beings can get into sex, the weird shit that they can do. "All that is can be gotten." The sex thing is related to the food thing. Animals don't care that much about sex as they do about eating. When I meditated at this one creek, I'd see these water birds, and they'd go for fish and just swallow the fish whole, feel the fish die in their body. Primitive. And down in Mexico before pre-Columbian times they'd cut a fuckin' human chest open, pluck out the heart real fast, and then hold it up, still beating in their hand, that's how fresh it was. Those people were completely intoxicated with that kind of stuff.

You mentioned a past lifetime. Can you tell us more about that?

Fjord was the guy I was in my past lifetime, a real heavy sadist, that's why his kid had epileptic fits. See, when you're young, that person from your previous life hasn't really died yet. And Fjord was really so much a part of me as a young person, it's like we were twins or something. He was a Norwegian silversmith.

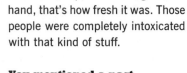

Maxon at home, cleaning the pyloric valve.

Photo © Anthony Petkovich

You're sure?
Definitely. There's no problem.

How did you come to realise a detail like that?
Well, the first awakening was some kind of hippie Ouija board thing back in the Seventies. The Ouija board said that I was a silversmith by the name of Fjord. That's all it told me. But if you super-psychoanalyse yourself really well, for years, accurately, and you're smart enough to really know what you're doing, you're going to come to a certain point where you realise reincarnation. And you're the person who can psychoanalyse you far better than anybody else because no matter how much you tell a doctor, you always know the truth yourself. And Fjord took over my body for a long time as a teenager.

When you're young, you do all kinds of weird things and you don't know why you do them. For instance, I smoked a pipe when I was a teenager. I didn't actually inhale, but I'd walk around with a pipe, because Fjord would walk along the cold Norwegian roads with a pipe. And even in deeper ways I could tell I was this guy Fjord. I worked on cars, I worked on metal. I just wanted to polish the metal because I was a silversmith doing fine work on metal. The trips my personality went through were so related to this guy.

But Fjord was a silversmith, a real good worker in Norway or one of those Scandinavian countries. And my get is that he had a kid who had seizures. And Fjord really worked at his trade, was good at it, made money off it, and with his money he bought this kid who had seizures. And Fjord would have these really strong experiences with women — mainly of a sadomasochistic nature — and these experiences caused Fjord's son to have these epileptic seizures. So if the kid had a seizure, Fjord would have this beautiful experience with a woman. It was this man and this kid playing this fuckin' game, bouncing this energy back and forth.

You say Fjord bought the kid?
Well, every parent buys their kid… every kid is every parent's slave. Even Charles was my old man's slave. But that's exactly what happens with the reproduction thing. It's a weird game, and a fact which society continues to erase. I mean, what does a person get when they get a kid? It's a responsibility, sure. But you get a human being that's all *yours*.

Anyhow, the broads would just come to Fjord and he'd work their fuckin' asses over for all they were worth. The guy wasn't even fucking them. He was heavy into sadism, knew exactly how to treat these really beautiful broads, and he treated 'em like fuckin' shit, and they would just get off on it, and he'd get off on it, and who would pay for it? His kid would pay for it by having an epileptic fit. And as long as Fjord had this kid, he had this power over women. So he consumed for two, ate both our beans.

But what happened in the long run was that the kid died in a funny situation. That was Fjord's crime: the fact that his kid died in the nuthouse. See, the kid kept going crazy and wound up in a mental institution, and something happened in the mental institution where some people tried to get some sort of homosexual thing out of him, and he had a *grand mal* fit and it killed him. And when the kid died, Fjord's trip was over, the whole thing just collapsed on him. Fjord's wife started running around with all the young bloods and getting real masochistic with them, and Fjord just couldn't tolerate it, so one fine day he took a revolver, went out into the woods, and committed suicide by either shooting himself in the head or the stomach. But, again, Fjord was responsible for that kid's death, and it set up the retribution, it set up all this bullshit that I was born with. It was really easy getting in touch with this past life person because I started doing it through the fucking seizures.

But your brother Charles also had some sort of power over you as a kid.
Charles hung so heavy, so bad over me as a kid that his dominance caused me to have seizures. He had that *over* me, man. I was in his power. So what you do is you kind of reverse the situation. That's why Charles killed himself… because there was a complete reversal of circumstance. There's always a reversal in life that turns things around. As a young man I was gettin' rid of Fjord. When I started having sex I was gettin' rid of him a lot. But before that time he really had a strong grip on me. It's almost like you're taken over by another spirit. I could just see that

This page Maxon Crumb art.
Next page Brother Robert comments on **Hardcore Mother** in a letter to Maxon.

guy in me. Then I started having sex, that changed me, I got a job, and I got into the world a bit. So I left a corpse back there of what this guy was.

You mentioned to me that you feel you were born under a bad sign or in a bad position, which would seem to lead back to Fjord's crime, right?
Right. When you psychoanalyse yourself, you'll come up with certain patterns in your lifetime because you were born in a certain position in relation to the other members of your family. And you were either born in a good or a bad position. Like my brother Charles was born in a really *good* position with my mother, whereas I was born in a really *bad* position with her.

So what happens is, when a person is born in a bad position or being punished for something... like when I was born, the situation was so bad it was like a jail sentence. So there are different positions. Like when a guy is a multi-millionaire, a big success in the movies, has tons of broads, or something like that... his life is good, he's got something going. There's a real palpable reason for that. He's in a *good* position. That *means* something. Another guy has just gone to jail for some stupid little crime, and he's on some fucking hideous San Quentin trip with all these people trying to fuck him in the ass and this bullshit... I mean, a *miserable* hell. And those are real fucking values.

So I was arbitrarily born in a bad position in the Crumb family, right? And you can say that yes, it started when I was born, when my first consciousness came to be. And some psychiatrist will go on about, "Oh, you fucked up your toilet training" and all this. But wait a minute, we're talking about a real quantity, so you must have done something wrong to be fuckin' punished. So you gotta go back. In other words, if we were born in a totally objective place, what would it be? If we were born without reincarnation, we would have to be born in some kind of virgin woods with no conditions, because you have to have a past if there was a condition. And Charles got my mother's adoration and I got none of that. She didn't like me. The real truth about my parents is that I was kind of removed from them. The real relationship I had was not with my parents but with my brothers and sisters. Charles was like my real father, which was some pretty heavy karma... it was pretty fucked up.

Before Charles' death, you two hadn't talked or communicated with one another for 20 years. What happened to cause such a long-term separation?
The funny thing about Charles is that he'd provoke you so bad, then if you tried to hit him, he'd just cover his head and burst out laughing because he knew you'd already blown all your control. He was a psychological terrorist as a kid. And, again, he actually started

C ... ... MUS OM TO H ... ... B 1 O GET N ...
OF IT, MAYBE IT'D BE A GOOD THING FOR YOU, I DON'T KNOW... FOR ME IT'S 7
MUCH AGGRAVATION TO EVEN THINK ABOUT...
    I OF COURSE HAVE READ THE STORY, 'HARD CORE MOTHER'... IT IS ONE OF
THE STRANGEST, QUIRKIEST PIECES OF LITERATURE I'VE EVER READ, I MUST ADMIT...
IT IS BIZARRE IN THE EXTREME... WELL-WRITTEN, INTERESTING, ENTERTAINING EVEN...
A BIT HARROWING... WHERE DO SUCH IDEAS COME FROM? WHERE DID THE IDEAS
COME FROM?? SOME NEWS ACCOUNT YOU FOUND IN A NEWSPAPER?? I THOUGHT IT
WAS VERY WELL-WRITTEN AND COHERENT, POSSIBLY EVEN "WORLD CLASS" LITERATURE...
BUT, AGAIN, ITS EXCEEDING STRANGENESS MAY IMPAIR ITS PUBLISHABILITY... I DON'T
KNOW... MAYBE YOU SHOULD GIVE OR SEND A COPY TO JON LONGHI AT LAST GASP...
    ANOTHER THING, WAS IT FINISHED? WAS THAT THE END?? (P.37)?
    ONE TECHNICAL CRITICISM AT THE BOTTOM OF PAGE THE NARRATION
METZURAY W MED TO PHYSICA UT HA
THE BEGINN
MOTHE

CRUMB

making me have seizures. It was so bad living with Charles that by the time I became a teenager and there were some kind of inclinations of sex, that's when I started having seizures because my mind could not accept sex or anything like that. Charles was just turning some fuckin' screw in me that just... (exhales deeply)... it's hard to say what. It's just so fucking subtle. The guy was just... you wouldn't believe what a sharp demon he was.

In Crumb, Robert points towards Charles' attraction to the young lad Jim Hawkins in Stevenson's Treasure Island.
Well, Charles was virgin all his life. He never had sexual intercourse because he basically had this thing about homosexuality. He was really attracted to little boys and stuff, and that's why he never had sex because he couldn't get what he wanted, and he didn't want to hurt any kids and go to jail. I had a few years of some kind of sex life, but it didn't work right because of my epilepsy. And then I gave up and had this religious thing. Robert had some kids and somewhat of a normal life, but also a kind of weird sex life... a sort of sado thing going on with women.

So in Charles' case, how was there a reversal of karma?
Well, he was a homosexual, but somehow my sister Sandra was able to turn it into shame on him. She humiliated him and he couldn't stand it because she was a woman —*and* she had kids. It was the same thing with Van Gogh. See, Van Gogh had this grip on his younger brother Theo and made him support him because Vincent was the mother's favourite. But when Theo met this woman, had sexual relations with her, and had children, all of that annihilated Theo's mind from being subjected to his mother's wishes, and Vincent had no other support or anything like that. And we had the same thing with my family.

Through Sandra's shaming of Charles?
Right. Sandra managed to turn Charles' domination over the rest of us around on him, and his mind just could not conceive such chronic reversal. It was so violent in his mind; that's why when his head was just screaming at him, he ended up trying to commit suicide. Again, the same thing happened to Van Gogh with the reversal that his brother put into place.

Would you mind talking more about Charles' suicidal tendencies?
Charles had a premonition that he was going to commit suicide, see. The first time he attempted to kill himself was in 1970. He was in his mid-twenties at the time. One night he went downstairs into the kitchen, and looked

Jim Hawkins (detail) in Treasure Island Days by Charles and Robert Crumb, 1959. © Robert Crumb under the sink where my mother kept certain chemicals to clean the house with. So he picked out a bottle of furniture polish from all these chemicals, and my mother half-way wakes up from falling asleep in front of the TV and says, "What the hell are you doing under there?", and he tells her very calmly, "I was fishing around for some type of poison to kill myself." And after breaking this to her, she just goes to sleep again. So he goes upstairs and does it.

And this all can be traced back to Sandra's shaming him.

Right. During Charles' run-in with my younger sister Sandra, she said something weird to Charles, and it flipped his head out, and his head started screaming that he wanted to kill. Constantly his head screamed. And I don't know how long it went on for, a couple months or something, and he just couldn't take it anymore and he got the furniture polish and drank it — glug! glug! glug! — then he went back up into his room, sat down in his chair, and some super LSD trip starts coming over him, and he starts seeing colours and the whole

Maxon's illustration for Poe's **The Raven**. Taken from **Maxon's Poe**. © Maxon Crumb

thing, gets scared shitless, and starts screaming for help. And my older sister Carol, who was visiting at the time, she heard him hollering, and went into his room to ask him what was wrong. And that's when he said he'd poisoned himself and was dying. And... sheesh!... oh, man... So they got him to the hospital and pumped his stomach and saved his life. And after he came out of the hospital he had to go back in again... he went into a coma for like four weeks or something. And he was in the nuthouse for a while.

But, all that pain aside, Charles was a big influence on both Robert and you, right?

Well, Robert used to say that a lot more than I did. But when I think back as I get older, Charles *really* made life exciting... because he was such a wacko character. We'd go off on these fucking adventures and it seems like we were living in some kind of fantasy world which most kids sort of don't have. During my childhood and Robert's childhood, Charles set the tempo. He was a character who just had no stability, who couldn't even know fear because he seemed to forget the ugly things that happened to him right away. And he'd end up doing this crazy stuff all the time. A real wacko character. And that's why he ended up living with my mother all the time because he just couldn't stand the world, because he was so wacko.

It's funny because you'd think Charles, of all the brothers, would be the one who'd really want to break away from the family and go on to bigger adventures.

Yeah, but he overloaded. It was too much for him, so he became a recluse. And a lot of people talk about my religious fanaticism, but Charles became religiously fanatic for a certain period with regard to literature. He had this little place down in the basement where he'd work all day, constantly writing stuff in these little notebooks where he would just copy down all the works of Shakespeare and Homer and Dickens. And after a while he got into some kind of spiritual trance doing that.

Now that several years have passed since the premiere of <u>Crumb</u>, looking back, how do you feel about the project as a whole?

I wasn't so much against the movie. I was kind of non-committal in a certain way. But I did *not* like the experience of filming it. It was real abrasive, almost like putting your body through a goddamn machine. It wasn't too bad when we were shooting in my hotel room, but when they tried to shoot Robert and me on Mission Street, that's when it really got self-conscious. The clip Terry has in the movie is of Robert and me walking along Mission Street and talking. And Robert and I had some nice bits between us, but every time we did a nice bit, the people doing the technical end would flub things up, make a mess of it. You can see remnants in the film of how Terry was trying to put some idea into Robert's head about Robert being disgusted with the cheap sell. So Terry dragged us down to Mission Street and we were supposed to be sitting there, talking about how awful all this cheap-sell crap is, which was a lame-ass idea, right? So then Robert just totally clams up. I mean, he really got self-conscious, and I'm supposed to talk to him and convince him about this subject matter, and I remember some street musician coming up to us and asking, "What're you guys filming?" And Robert just says to him, "Don't worry about it. You'll never see this film." (Laughs) I think *all* of us thought nothing much was going to come out of it.

Terry, of course, was a little upset that he wasn't nominated for an Academy Award, but that's all political. The trouble is that he wasn't popular with the industry because he had a big hit out of nowhere and copped some of the industry's market and all that shit. (Laughs)

This page Panels from "I Remember The Sixties: R. Crumb Looks Back!", <u>**Weirdo No 4**</u>. © Robert Crumb
Next page Self-portrait by Robert for the cover of <u>**Self-Loathing Comics No 1**</u>. © Robert Crumb

Can you fill us in on Robert's early work as a commercial artist? That

part seems sort of glossed over in the movie.

Well, for his first drawing job, he went to Cleveland and showed his drawings to these people in some kind of employment agency or something, and they could see that the guy was pretty advanced, so they sent him over to American Greeting Cards, and those guys gave him a job in colour separation. It was real meticulous and boring work, but he only had to stay in that department for eight or nine months or something. And he had this one cubicle-desk in what seemed like a huge hall of cubicle-desks... very Kafkaesque... and this guy would walk down the aisle between the rows of cubicles and make sure you were working real hard. Mass production painting. That was around the time he did the Big Yum Yum Book [*Editor's note: Big Ass Comics, perhaps? I don't think there was a comic by the name of Big Yum Yum Book*], which really shows his terrible horniness. Robert was an extremely repressed guy for a long time as a teenager. Dangerously repressed. And he was pretty sex-starved at that time in Cleveland... wasn't gettin' any. He used to send me these weird letters with detailed descriptions from news articles in which women were brutally raped by gangs of blacks. (Laughs) He was in a pretty spooky spot. But he was also working his ass off.

And he told me much later that the company actually sent him to school for a while where they tell you *exactly* how they want you to do these fucking greeting cards. As far as what sells, they had the things down to a science. You had to draw all the people in the cards as kind of pudgy and bland. And, you know, Robert liked to draw things that were more morbid, with clutching fingers and gnarled hands. But they didn't want him to do that. But eventually they allowed him to develop his own kind of style. Man, I thought he had the poshest job in the world.

But every once in a while he would just take off from the job, get out, hitchhike around, go to New York or Chicago, and just wouldn't go back to work. He'd just disappear. Then he'd eventually go back to work, and his wife would go patch it up with the greeting card company. And, I mean, the people at his work just put up with this stuff. (Laughs) Then everything was happening in California with the hippies, and the flower children, and the drugs, and all that, and he became somewhat of an acid freak during this period. He'd go to New York City into a dive hotel, and start taking all this acid, and having these incredible trips with himself, right there in the room. Super scroungy hotels in New York. And somehow he plugged into that LSD period, and it went to his fucking head in some kind of crazy way where he dug stuff so far back from his head, from his memory... it really whacked my head out because I'd seen all that shit... it was buried in my unconsciousness, too.

See, the family thing was just such an intense mess, you know. (Laughs) There was so much of this struggle with my intense epileptic thing, my religious thing, my mother had all these problems with drugs, Charles attempted suicide a number of times, and somehow Robert had some kind of karma whereby he was able to translate all this stuff generated from that family situation into a personal kind of success. I'm not saying he did anything wrong, or even intended anything wrong. He was not the type of guy that really cared. He's not a hustler. All this crazy stuff regarding his success just hap-

pened all at once. There was no logic involved. Absolutely no logic.

From what I read about Robert after the film's release, he had quite a problem with the publicity generated towards him.
Yeah. Robert just hates the publicity. After the film came out, he did that whole thing where he grew long hair, grew a beard, and now he wears different clothes.

So he became a hippie.
He doesn't look like a hippie now. He looks more like Dostoevsky or Solzhenitsyn. He's got this beard and his hair's thinning slightly on top... it's this new look, like a Russian thinker or something. And he looks okay that way. It's a new phase for him... it's like his 'old man' phase. If you look at certain pictures of him when he started to get famous, he's like this young man coming out. And after the big explosion happened in the Seventies, he started looking like a middle-aged businessman, like Groucho Marx or something. (Laughs) But now he's got this Russian thinker thing going on.

What about the Poe book? Did you read the Poe stories immediately before doing the artwork for each?
I hadn't read "Valdemar" before, and that was a real treat, an excellent story. "The Raven" I've always been reading, so that was no problem. And "The Tell Tale Heart"... as kids, before going to sleep at night, when Robert, Charles and I were bedding in the same room, Charles would often recite "The Tell Tale Heart" by memory, from start to finish. I was like 11 or 12 at the time. I remember one time Charles was drunk and doing the ghost of Hamlet. Man, he did a beautiful job. He was about 20, and he had a sheet over him, and was climbing the stairs with a candle, reciting those lines. Put Barrymore to shame, man. And when he got to the top of the stairs, doing this heavy Shakespeare thing, he just toppled back, falling down the stairs... (laughs)... probably on purpose.

You're off the welfare now, right?
Yeah. I dumped the welfare. I was on it for a looooong time. (Laughs) Now 'art' is my job. (Laughs) The whole thing is partially about trying to make money, but also about not turning yourself into a whore. And while you've gotta allow yourself some time to get promoted, it does occasionally feel as if you're whoring yourself.

But the money thing's not too scary at the moment because my agent has some money coming in from gallery sales. And hopefully the Poe book will do well. But, still, there's no logic to it. Like this thing with the welfare. See, all these people started approaching me when this movie came out, right? I mean, it fucked up my income because this thing, this *movie* kept insisting and insisting and insisting, and money started really coming in so I *had* to dump welfare. But it's so illogical. I really can't answer right now whether I wish the film ever came out or not. Maybe I was better off before it came out. (Laughs) I don't know. Maybe not. It's all relative. I mean, people come up to you at book signings thinking you're some kind of celebrity, but all you find are implications of another kind of anonymity. You get a little bit of fame, but then you see there's a whole larger market you can be in, but you're not; so, in relation to that larger market, you're really just fucking anonymous. (Laughs)

How were you raised by way of religion?
I was raised Catholic, our whole family was Catholic. And as a teenager I became some-what interested in the cultural end of the Catholic Church. It's an interesting religion

because the Catholic Church had these real medieval origins. And if you look at early painting, at early art... one of the greatest painters — one of the most interesting ones, at least — is Bruegel the Elder. When Bruegel was in the Netherlands, Spain had annexed the Netherlands, moved in on the Dutch, took 'em over for a while, and laid this real heavy Catholic thing on 'em, see. They were trying to break away from the Church at that time. Germany had already broken away. And the English were breaking away. But the Spanish had gotten hold of the Dutch. So that's why in Bruegel you have this real intense knowledge of death and a real intense understanding of persecution. He was tellin' the fuckin' truth in his stuff.

What about begging? Why did you begin that practice?
It's really tied into the whole vegetarian trip. Back in the mid-Seventies, I was attacked four times with guns and once with a knife within the course of a year, so I became a vegetarian — and the attacks against me stopped. You have to understand, the one basic purpose of human society is to cover their tracks when it comes to eating meat. In the natural environment, you kill the animal to eat its flesh, and the animal tries to kill you. But what human society basically joins together and does is cover over their consumption of meat, and they do so mainly by fighting wars. Bernard Shaw said the same thing. Everybody in India knows this shit. Human beings are the only creatures really capable of breaking the food chain. They're *conscious* enough to say, "I will not *willingly* eat this meat because I don't need it to survive." But so few human beings make that decision. Eating is much heavier than fucking.

And after these gun attacks came my way this one year, I figured there was definitely something wrong. So one morning I just went out and begged. Something in my head said, "Just go out and ask somebody for spare change. That will stop the guns." And the next morning I went out and did it. Some guy was coming along and I said, "Mister, can you spare some change so I can buy food?" And he gave me some money. So I just went back and bought some breakfast. And after a while I started making money from this sort of begging and being able to buy enough food to get me through to the next day.

When did the practice of meditation start meshing with your begging?
Well, after I started pretty much surviving off the begging, then I started to *find* food — a loaf of bread or some fuckin' thing. It's the karma... you don't have any money so the food just *comes* at you. And I was finding food so rapidly it almost got to the point where I was wondering if I was stealing it or something. (Laughs) So that's when I decided to sit in meditation and put the bowl down, because it was more controlled. I would go downtown to the Financial District in San Francisco — which is better than the Mission District because you can make more money — pick a spot, roll the rug out, put my legs in the lotus position which is really strong control, put the bowl out, and just wait for people to put money into it. And that's what pulled the whole thing down. I began making enough money for food and all that stuff, so I started to live that way.

And you also practice fasting, right?
Right. Fasting does a shitload of stuff to you. You get high, you get into different spiritual states... it definitely helps with my art. When I began practising meditation, I hadn't gotten locked into any fasting period yet. Then I had this dream where I was in a Zen monastery, and this Zen master comes up to me and says, "So you like to play chess, huh? We in the Orient have a certain way of playing chess. I'll show you." So we go to this counter, and the Zen master taps upon it, and this cook comes out and slams two bowls of

rice down upon the counter. And then the Zen master picks up a bowl, eats the rice really fast, and says, "Now *you* eat that bowl of rice and see if you can eat it faster than I ate mine." So I ate it really fast. Then he taps on the counter again, the cook brings out two more bowls of rice, and the master says, "Okay, now take a bowl and see how *slowly* you can eat it." (Laughs) So a couple of months later I went through this thing where I would take this bowl of rice and eat little bits of it. And I got really smacked out on that. You can really go on a spiritual ride with that kind of stuff. So I'd eat a bowl of rice in a day, and then later stretched it out to a day and a half.

At one point in <u>Crumb</u> we see you with a string of cloth dangling from your mouth. Can you explain that practice a bit?
Well, it's actually practical application. You do it because of the strict vegetarian diet. The cloth makes it possible not to eat meat. It's very low dye, fairly finely woven cotton, about 21 feet in length. And it basically takes about three days to come out the back, depending upon how fast you eat it. I do the cloth every six weeks, usually for about three or four days. But every couple of days I put a little bit of cloth in my stomach, just take a little bit that's six-feet long, swallow it, and leave it in the stomach for about two hours.

So why do you do it?
To clean the pyloric valve. And I always use this analogy to explain the reasoning behind it: one time I was walking down this road and I walked past an old farm house. And there was an old clothes line tied to one corner of the farm house, and on the end of that line was a rag. The house was next to an open field, it was windy, and the rag was all shredded from blowin' and bangin' against the side of the house. And where that rag was hittin' the side of the house, you could see that the cloth had worn down the paint at that spot, right down to bare wood. And it's basically the same thing with the cloth — you live with it for three days, and the movement of your body causes the cloth to rub against and clean your pyloric valve. See, the inside of your body is raw flesh. And this raw flesh excretes a mucous membrane, especially when you're eating food. It's like a lubricant or protective agent. And when you eat meat, the meat is just as heavy as the mucous membrane and it pushes it on through, or a good slug of milk will push it on through. But when you eat vegetarian food, it's very difficult to move that shit through… it gets bogged down. So you have to use this cloth which loosens it all up and helps push it along.

Maxon today
Photo © Anthony Petkovich

Let's talk a bit about mom and dad. Your father was a pretty tough character, wasn't he?
Well, like a lot of parents back then, my father would give us whippings when we were little kids. He always used to take me and Robert and Charles to the barber shop on the military base and get

these fucking haircuts that were (moves imaginary electric razor from back of his head to top) *bzzzzzzzzzzt!* (Laughs). We were in grade school at the time, so when you showed up for school on Monday, all the kids would be ribbin' you about being bald and stuff. As I got *so* fed up with the deal one time, that after I got the buzz, I said that I wasn't going to school. See, my mother would take us to

Early Crumbs.
Brothers (L–R) Maxon, Robert, and Charles.

school in the morning, and on this one particular morning I just wouldn't get out of the car. I had this haircut and I was just *not goin'*. (Laughs)

So did your dad beat the shit out of you when he got home that night?
Well, my mother tried to pull me out of the car, and when she failed she was like, "Ok-a-a-ay! You're going to get a beating from your father." So I didn't go to school that day. I mean, usually I was a really neat little kid. But once in a while I was a real stickler. So my dad was going to give a spanking, right? But I thought it out: 'Okay. He's going to give me a spanking. But I'm *not* going to cry. I'm not going squeal. I'm not going to make *one* sound. I'm gonna be in complete control of myself so that when he starts beating me, I'm just going to be totally cold.' And when he did start whacking away, I just... *nothin'*, you know. And then... he just gave up (snaps fingers) like that. And that's the last time I got a beating as a kid. I just thought it out. You cry and all that stuff, but when you do that, that's the worst part of it. How much is it really gonna hurt you? You're playing as a kid, and you fall halfway down a canyon wall, and your knee is all scraped and shit, and you get up and run away. I mean, *that* don't hurt anymore than getting a beating, does it?

But I wasn't really a very pushy kid. One time in Catholic school, though, I had this ball in my hand and a nun's back was turned and I just *beaned* her with that fuckin' thing in the back of the head. (Laughs) Blam! Knocked her fucking veil right off. And when she turned around I just said, "Oh Jesus, Sister. I'm really sorry." (Laughs) "I didn't mean to hit you. I was supposed to throw it over to — whatever kid — and my arm slipped accidentally... " She believed me, too. Most of the time I was a really docile kid who thought respect should be given to the adults. But as for beaning Sister Raymond Joseph, I think it was because there was so much sexual energy among those nuns... it really attracted me.

What about the molestations? How is it that you got into that particular scene?
Molestation is terribly fun. And I'm sure guys who are honest with themselves have at least *thought* about grabbing a woman's ass in an elevator, in a bar, or some more public place.

When did you start doing it?

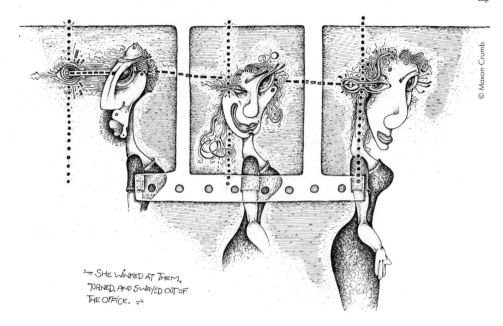

= SHE WINKED AT THEM, TURNED, AND SWAYED OUT OF THE OFFICE. =

In Philadelphia in the late-Sixties, when I was about 19. It was on some crowded subway train or something. There was this good-looking white chick, and I grabbed her tit I think. She pulled away and when the train stopped I just jumped right off. I did it again in the Seventies for a few years. And then in the Eighties I started getting into trouble with the law.

Why did you start molesting women in the first place?
I was fucked up about sex. Sometimes I'd meet some woman to see if I could get something going, but it was *so* stifling. Such a mess. You get a network of psychological hang-ups and fuck-ups that's so *large* that you could never get through it. It's like some big web of bushes or knotted leaves and trees, and you can never get through all this... 'growth' of psychological nightmares to just connect with a woman.

So you just admit it to yourself that you're inhibited. You can't *do* this thing with your body, so you simplify it. For instance, take the knob on this door. Now no matter what kind of hang-ups I have, I can still *touch* that knob. It's simple. Now here's a broad in the subway, right? And I like... *touch* her tit. (Laughs) It's simple. You just take your hand and make it... *do* it. You break down all the conditions. Grab a door knob, grab a tit — it's the same thing. And the broads really encourage it because they get a cheap fuckin' thrill out of it.

Can you set up a typical Maxon molestation for us?
I used to do a lot of it right off Union Square up on Stockton Street where there used to be lots of airline ticket offices and shit. The offices were upstairs, and I remember this little long hallway — kind of nicely done, with mirrors, new carpet, and metallic moulding — which would lead to an elevator. And, see, when you molest, you *do* stalk. You behave like a hunter. And there's a game involved. I mean, when you're really into a crime like that, you really get into the sense of 'field', and the victim plays ball with the criminal — there's no doubt about it. (Laughs) Some of them aren't even really conscious of it. Some are. But you do follow them, and most of them play right into your hands.

16

So you follow them into these intimate little places, then you'd just take the bottom of a broad's dress, which is usually real tight on the butt, and pull it up... (makes pulling motion with both hands)... Shoo! And at a certain point, when the dress gets over a certain curvature of the ass and hips, it like... pops out! Sometimes I'd call it "pheasant under glass" because a lot of these broads didn't have any clothes underneath their dress, or you could see their ass through the transparent nylons they'd be wearing.

Tell us about a woman who quite obviously liked being molested.
Well, there was this nice little Oriental broad in her early twenties, not very tall, and I keyed in on her. I followed her into one of these intimate hallways, and she was totally unaware. I can't remember what she was even *dressed* in, or what she looked like until *after* I pulled her dress up. And after I pulled it up, I saw that she didn't have any panties on. And at that point she just stuck this fuckin' pose like she was in a fuckin' porn scene or something... just stickin' her butt out. She just loved it. And then she looked at me, and in this real amusing little voice said (in slurred, effeminate voice), "*What* are you trying to do?" I've never heard someone say "no" in such an inviting way. (Laughs) Yeow. Anyhow, I obviously did *exactly* what she wanted. Then I just snapped right out of there.

How did these molestations eventually come to an end?
(Laughs) It took them a *long* time to catch me. They had many complaints at Macy's (Department Store). And with Macy's I really got heavy into getting *into* the store, getting deep into the place, up several floors, pulling a number, and getting out. You really gotta get *out* once you do that stuff. (Laughs) That was in the early-Eighties. But a place like Macy's is just like some big... ass emporium or somethin'. Broads just really enjoy getting dressed up and buying clothes and perfume and shit. They just *like* that. And after a while I started dressing in a certain way that was good for molesting... somewhat nondescript. I wouldn't wear something like this (indicates his own tunic) because people could mark you, it would be too obvious. So I'd just wear a regular shirt and a dark blue blazer, and a lot of times I could feel the broads bouncing off me as if I was one of the dicks or cops working for the house. And after a while you could just tell (laughs) when they stole something because I'd be looking at them funny, and they'd look at me funny thinking I was a cop, and you could just *tell* the ones who had stolen something. There was just the magnetism between the two of you.

And how were you caught?
A bunch of store detectives in Macy's jumped me right in the middle of the second floor, brought me downstairs and all this bullshit. But they really didn't do anything to me. They just dropped the fuckin' charges. I mean, I didn't expose her or anything. I think I just put my thumb up her ass or something. And she had a *real* nice ass. This broad liked it. She also liked the fact that I got jumped — she liked all the action, all the attention, all the drama... she just *loved* that stuff. The had me handcuffed, and they were leading me to this place, and she was just grinnin' back at me like I was some kind of fuckin' movie star. (Laughs)

How did the molestations balance themselves out with your karma?
By getting into fights all the time with cops, getting into fights on the street... I really got into negative karma from all that molestation shit. It's not always directly related, but it is karma, it does come back. You *know* it comes back. And when I got into molestation in the Eighties, I got so heavy into playing this karma game, it was like moving chess pieces. "Oh, I'll grab this one's ass, and this guy's going to come out, so I can step by on that one, and there's the cops on this one, and I really had a great time with her. Oh wow!" The women definitely dug it. The problem is the police didn't. (Laughs) So I couldn't help but

get into tons of trouble with cops. I spent two weeks in a psychiatric ward on haldol, a psychiatric drug, and anybody who *doesn't* get cured of any crime after they're incarcerated is just a fucking idiot. When you're incarcerated you learn to stop doing self-destructive shit to yourself. Jail's pretty bad, but the nuthouse is worse. They put you on heavy drugs in the nuthouse which is far worse than being behind bars because it's all *inside* you.

What about your epileptic seizures? Have you ever sought out medical help for your affliction?

The Western approach to epilepsy is all fucked up. First of all, the seizures are a religious fucking thing, but Western medicine just refuses to deal with them as such. I mean, if I was in India having these seizures, they'd put me in a temple as a holy man. But here they want to pump drugs into you and cut up your brain. They talk about nuthouses, but the patients who occupy them, and the people who *administer* them are both nuts. One is masochistic, while the other one is sadistic. It's all fucked up. One person is crazed because they *want* the fucking shock treatment. The other person is crazed because they *give* the fucking shock treatment

Would a porn film throw you into an epileptic fit?

If I sat there and really looked at it for about half an hour or so, yeah, I'd just go right into a fit. That's why I can't go to any nude dance clubs. Just seeing a girl with exposed tits would probably get me going. Even if she just came in here and started dancing in front of me in the nude (snaps his fingers) I'd go right into a seizure.

So when you do 'make it big', do you think you'll ever give up the begging?

When people become famous, I think it has something to do with their past lifetime... they've paid some kind of dues. Like in wars where people are killed... the Nazis killing all those Jews... all the murder, execution, and atrocities in history. All those corpses have to be paid back, you know.

But, no, I'll never give up the begging. It's part of my life, part of my karma, and there's nothing I can do about it. ◉

the grotesque burlesque

An evening in the company of the Dragon Ladies and friends

David Kerekes

 e start this little journey in a dream I had the night before. There I am sitting in an old school hall, struggling to manoeuvre those steel and plastic chairs that are hooked up together. Then the Bonzo Dog Doo Dah Band begin to play. It's a chaotic show that includes tall buildings live on stage and several shifts in the dream space/time continuum. I'm trying to write a review of the show, but then I get beaten up…

The Dragon Ladies call themselves "a cult art troupe". Of the three-piece, Marisa Carr may be familiar to readers for her organisation of the first UK Smut Fest back in 1994 (see headpress 10), while Adrian Jones was once a member of the band Rancho Diablo (see headpress 11). Amanda Moss, the third member of the troupe, we had never met or spoken to before.

Our invitation to see the Dragon Ladies show, *The Grotesque Burlesque*, arrives. It is to be staged at the Raymond Revuebar Theatre in Soho, Sunday 8th February 1998. Also on the bill for the evening are Snowpony, Jake Vegas, and a film show by Jason Wilcox.

Cut to the present. I'm making my way over to the Raymond Revuebar. David Slater, who I've travelled down to London with for this occasion, is being propositioned by a prostitute. "Forty quid?" she asks. He shakes his head. She drops the price by 10 pounds. It's Sunday and it's late. Dave's still not interested, so she moves on, back to her pimp in the shadows. A minute or two earlier, just round the corner, we almost end up in the wrong Revuebar. That could have been entertaining, I suppose, sitting in a dimly lit theatre waiting for the *Grotesque Burlesque* to start. "*Is this it?*" we could have pondered as some dodgy-looking bird wobbled her breasts for us. But the lady on the door was very honest. It obviously pained her to lose two prospective customers, but we charmed her with a smile and she admitted that this place wasn't actually *the* place. As we waved her goodbye, we promised we would return later. We don't.

So we find the Raymond Revuebar as a drunk starts to take a piss in the doorway opposite. (He's quickly sent on his way.) We hand in our tickets at the door, pick up a couple of beers, and make our way up to the auditorium.

Before long every seat in the place is taken.

Smoking is permitted, but no one smokes. No one says much, either. I for one am sitting in silence. For a World Famous Club, I'm struck by how small the stage is.

The lights go dim and a pulsating Moog hum fills the air. The satin curtain rises and on stage stand four motionless female figures, all wearing face masks. They have their backs to the audience, but their masks face forward. They remind me of Pompeii I saw as a child: men, women and animals petrified by lava, their limbs askew for eternity.

This is the Nightmare Chorus Line and it stands unmoving for a very long time. Prosthetics enhance the female physique to Chesty Morgan-like proportions. Suddenly, the pounding of a slow, lazy drumbeat cuts through the air — with a bassline straight out of a Tempest Storm show reel — and the figures begin a slow syncopated dance. Only it's not a dance as such, the Chorus Line simply jerk their arms and heads awkwardly from one side to the other. For several minutes they do this, their unblinking expressionless gaze fixed into the auditorium. I feel a warm glow of unease. The music fades. The curtain falls.

And so the stage is set. This is the *Grotesque Burlesque*.

Next to make an appearance is Dolly Blue. Despite her big tattoos, stained complexion, heaving bosom and open vagina with teeth and leering tongue, Dolly has the demeanour of a sweet young thing. She flutters her eyelids at the audience and takes tiny tippy-toe steps from one end of the stage to the other. Her musical accompaniment is a carnival waltz, jolly and sinister.

In one of the show's few spoken word pieces, we hear the tale of old sea dog Captain Blue, who marries dainty Dolly. Together they set sail in a ship called, conveniently and confusingly enough, the *Dolly Blue*. Once at sea, however, plague and temptation undermine the marriage, and things for the newly weds soon go bad. Bluebeard says to Dolly:

On your knees, whore. Dirty whore. Bloody whore. I see your scarlet stained hands, you disobeyed my wishes, wife. And now the roses weep tears of blood for you. Caught red-handed, harlot… my doll. My Dolly Blue. Your character betrayed you, love, and now your role is finally cast. Calm yourself. Woman be willing in your whorish heart. Die for the sins of your kind. Hush, little one… little baby girl. Silence your tongue. This is how it will be done. I will cover you in porcelain and carve you at the knees, and place you as a figurehead against the raging seas. Dolly Blue… Dolly Blue… sealed forever in your own horrific humour. So, suffer for me, pretty. Suffer for me, sweet… as I rip out your throat and cut off your feet.

What Dolly is supposed to have done to incur such wrath, I am not sure. But we're not talking chronological narrative here, anyway. The story progresses making no pretence to differentiate between what is real and what is not. Allegory and myth ride the coat-tail of a fine, fiery musical score.

Dolly Blue is murdered by the Captain (in a roundabout, ethereal way), has her limbs hacked off and turned into a human figurehead for his ship. Enter the frame Violet Rose, a strange horned Kali-like sea creature who dances an Eastern kind of dance. Her movements one minute are wooden and brusque; the next they are all over the place, rapid and hysterical, like a soul possessed. Violet Rose dies, too, replaced by Bloody Pearl, who eventually picks herself up and wanders blankly from the stage into the audience, bringing the show to a close.

Woman as victim, woman as goddess, woman as Camille Keaton in the final moments of *I Spit on Your Grave*.

The *Grotesque Burlesque* draws on elements of Music Hall, Chinese Theatre, the *Rime of the Ancient Mariner* and, I'm sure, a whole bunch of other stuff. But my mind through the performance is turned off to reason and conjecture. From those opening moments in the Nightmare Chorus Line, I want nothing more than to bathe in the withered grip on reality that the show promises.

And it's a withered grip aided immeasurably by the fact that the three female characters — Dolly Blue, Violet Rose and Bloody Pearl — are all played by the same person, Marisa Carr. Indeed, with the exception of a few peripheral souls — notably a Tattooed Sailor and a Demonic Child — these are the only characters in the whole performance. With Marisa up on stage alone for almost the entire duration of the show (close on one hour), it is no mean feat that she is able to command attention and not allow the *otherworldliness* to slip for a moment.

But it's far from being a solo effort. The bulbous-vagina costumes and designs by Amanda Moss, and music by Adrian Jones, are the foundation to this *nether dimension*.

The end of the *Grotesque Burlesque* doesn't herald the end of the night's entertainment. A guy called Jake Vegas does a spot as DJ and plays a live "rootsy" set in the upstairs bar. We see none of his routine, however (his name puts us off). Instead, in the hour before Snowpony take to the stage, Dave and myself go for a wander through some of the book and video emporiums around Soho. Then to a pub for a beer.

Snowpony. L–R Katharine, Max, Deb.

"IT SEEMS THE BACKLASH HAS ALREADY BEGUN. The SUNDAY PEOPLE ran a story this week expressing outrage at the use of lottery funds to promote a 'KINKY DANCE ACT'. Of course they hadn't actually seen the show, and we had refused to talk to them... The notion of the work being based on a FEMALE REINTERPRETATION of a traditional fable driven by FEMININE POWERS and featuring PREDATORY SEXUAL FEMALES utterly in control of their circumstances seems too difficult and, possibly, terrifying for quite a number of people to accept. It's far easier for them to reduce the whole piece to the level of pandering to male fantasy and exploitation."

—Adrian Jones

Snowpony are a three-piece band who utilise tape loops along with a live bass, drum and vocal line-up. As opposed to being 'backing' filler, as is so often the case with tapes, these are loops which create peculiar little counterpoints in the performance. They're often playing on a different time signature to the live rhythm section, which makes for a hypnotic, sometimes fragile, sometimes antagonistic, sound. Snowpony trigger several (unintentional) musical moments from one of my all-time favourite obscure bands: the Mexican prog rocksters, Aguaturbia. I don't really know why. Maybe there is a touch of South of the Border in those loops somewhere (there's certainly some heavy guitar shunting).

For the last number in the Snowpony set, several members of the *Burlesque* troupe — including one lady who stubs a cigarette out on her tongue — get up and gyrate.

All of which leaves little time for Jason Wilcox, the film show man. Things are running late. His compilation of film clips — which purport to reflect the themes inherent in the Dragon Ladies' show — starts to roll when Jason is still making his introductory talk. He does manage a few disembodied words in the darkness, however.

The clips are taken from movies by directors such as Jean Rollin, Harry Kumel and Walerian Borowczyk. When all mental faculties are fresh and alert that's a pretty lethal combination — right now, close on midnight, it's the most terrible thing either one of us can think of.

The following morning Dave and myself trek halfway across London for an egg sandwich in our favourite London café. The two-hour-long walk is supposed to help clear our heads, but I can't wait to eat so that I might down a couple of Nurofen tablets. Afterwards we make our way to Euston station for the return train home. First, however, I make a detour into the Virgin Megastore on Oxford Street in search of Snowpony platter. I go to the Help Desk, but in my drunken stupor insist on calling the band *Snow Goose*. The guy taps into his computer every permutation of the words Snow and Goose but, fortunately, nothing comes back. (I might have ended up with a Rick Wakeman album!) Some days later, having realised my mistake, I trawl Manchester's independent record shops inquiring after Snowpony. Still no joy.

Eventually, through the band themselves, I land a copy of the 'Easy Way Down' single. (See page 95.)

AMANDA MOSS

The Dragon Ladies.
Image-maker and installations.

How did it all start?

The Dragon Ladies formed in 1997. Prior to that we had already worked together — Marisa, myself and Adrian —with Rancho Diablo, who were doing a gig at the Monarch. We did a piece set to some of their music. That was the first time Marisa performed in the prosthetic skins. We then went on to do our separate things. When we found ourselves free in January, we decided to get together in a more 'official' capacity. We applied for the Chisenhale Dance Space commission, which was for dance and the extraordinary, and we were lucky enough to get it and that's how the show was created.

Was the Dragon Ladies something that each of you envisaged? Was that the way each of you wanted to go?

Marisa has been performing for a long time. Adrian was making experimental music, and I was working on images and working in photography. We thought, we've worked together before, and we like the element of fusing all of these disciplines together and mixing high and low art. We all wanted to mix all our talents together and see what came out.

What comes first: your designs or the show?

I think it all happens together. The way we worked on the show was that I had been thinking about this idea of a 2,000-year-old woman — Bloody Pearl — and I wanted to make a full-body tattooed skin. We had that image and we had some music… The background of who she was all came about pretty simultaneously: Marisa wrote a ballad. We kind of worked backwards from the last image. Backwards and forwards — it's a very composite type of way that we work.

Why do the characters have such huge vaginas?

That's a direct result of my years of work as a developing artist, which led me to focus on fe-male subject matter — more specifically certain areas of the body. I have tried to investigate a new female symbolism and explore the way that these symbols are displayed in culture. My main references have been to examine breasts, vaginas and the skin. The devices I use to place emphasis on these parts is to exaggerate and mutate the ordinary meaning into something fantastic and mythological.

My previous work used photography to capture these notions of female sexuality, in a collection of characters which formed what I called the "Mutant Wife Series", in 1994. You may well be seeing some sort of return to these more naturalistic vaginal representations in future Dragon Ladies shows.

What was the criteria for the other acts involved in the show?

We've performed the show three times, and we applied for a lottery grant. And what we wanted to do was promote cutting edge performance, music, and give space to artists who perhaps couldn't find the right forums in the traditional sense, like in an art gallery, or in theatre.

Jason Wilcox… when we did the Oxton Hall show, I think it was, he actually phoned the studio because he was researching everything he could possibly research about dragons. He goes to this radical anthropology group, which Marisa and myself now attend regularly. And he gave this whole other context to the mythology we deal with, and put it into context of mythic thought. He's always coming to us with books and things. He has a pretty good understanding of what we're doing. The film show was his idea of how he saw the show, from an anthropological viewpoint.

I didn't know he was interested in Dragons?

Yeah. I think in the Yellow Pages it says 'Dragon Ladies', and he rung up and said "Dragon Ladies, what's that about because I'm really interested in dragons?"

An entry in the Yellow Pages for The Dragon Ladies?!
Yes, I guess it was.

Anyone else phone up?
Only people trying to sell us double glazing.

● ● ● ● ● ● ● ● ● ● ● ● ● ● ● ● ● ● ● ●

ADRIAN JONES

The Dragon Ladies.
Music.

Is Rancho Diablo no more?
Yeah, it died a horrible death about a year ago. A clash of creative differences and egos. I knew Marisa at the time the band was going, and knew that she was out on her fucked-up performance trip — where we wanted to go as a band — and thought she'd be excellent and very appropriate for the music we were doing. And she did actually perform a number of times with us to one of our numbers. Amanda was designing the gear that Marisa was wearing… That's how the Dragon Ladies association started, and basically we figured that this was such a unique way of working that we ought to purify it and just do that alone, as opposed to being a side-piece to what the band was doing.

How much of a role does your music play in the actual writing and choreography?
It depends really. Sometimes I'll come up with a piece of music that'll then be choreographed to, or the narrative overlaid on that. Other times there's a routine that needs a very specific routine or structure. This depends on what stage we're all at. Very often Marisa has a script worked out, and I have a piece of music and she'll fit that into the music.

The opening Nightmare Chorus Line couldn't have existed without that particular piece of music, and in a way it is that which sets the tone for the whole show.
Yeah. Originally that existed as a big up-beat orchestral striptease number. It's a piece that originally only occurred mid-way through the show, and we only decided later to put it on at the beginning as well, to set the tone, and announce the Dragon Ladies arrival at the Raymond Revuebar! We needed a big band number to kick the doors in, as it were.

It would have been great if you'd stuck that music on, unannounced, for a normal mid-week Revuebar audience!
I don't think they'd have known what to make of it to be honest.

How do you construct a piece of work?
I spend long hours in a little room absorbed in all sorts of weird samples, loops, driving myself mad with sea shanties and nursery rhymes. Particularly with this production. There's a lot of repetition of very simple structures and it's quite disorientating after a while. Fairgrounds — that's the sort of imagery I'm trying to evoke.

● ● ● ● ● ● ● ● ● ● ● ● ● ● ● ● ● ● ● ●

MARISA CARR

The Dragon Ladies.
Scriptwriter and choreographer.

When we last spoke, at the Smut Fest in 1994, you said you wanted to put burlesque into a smoky environment.
I don't really have a policy now, like 'art should be here, art should be there'. But I do like the idea we're putting this into a proper burlesque theatre that is built for the burlesque art.

Who is Dolly Blue?
Dolly Blue is a character we created. From my part it was coming from looking at the old music hall ladies in the East End, and also looking at the character of my grandmother, who was a bit of an East End old Jewish lady. Dolly Blue is a bawdy, blue showgirl, but she's also like a China

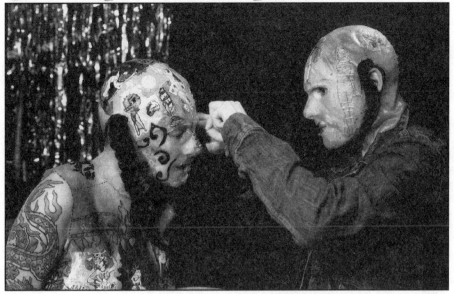

Amanda Moss (right) applying grotesque makeup to Marisa Carr.
Photo © Paulinia Portugal / Dragon Ladies

doll; naïve and breakable. And a peacock — a very elegant, feminine-looking bird that's actually a male. Both male and female at the same time; and funny and whorish. It's kind of playing with the whole showgirl thing. Dolly Blue is parading female sexuality with a kind of male aggression.

When you think of music hall, you don't exactly think of younger people being at all interested. It's more old folk reminiscing. Why does it interest you?

I'm just really interested in entertainment traditions, melodrama, and extreme theatre traditions. If you look at British music hall, the women who performed in it were young, and singing these really rude sexual songs. They were actually very political, too. Marie Lloyd, for instance, refused to do the Royal Command Performance, and she wanted to legalise prostitution. It all becomes glossed over, like, *the good old days*, nice and funny. But the music halls in reality were where all the prostitutes, pimps, and pushers hung out. It was a very subversive, radical place. It was low-class entertainment; the equivalent of strip clubs and gigs today. It was the end of the last century when Marie Lloyd was at her peak, and that's where most of the characterisa-

tion of Dolly Blue comes from. I'm fascinated by the *look* of that era, the evocative dressing for the stage. We always think of Victorian England as prim, and in denial of sexuality, but if you look a little further into Victorian working class culture, it's really upfront and raunchy. It's a rich history that says a lot about the psychology and about class in society.

There is a real nightmare element to the show. What draws you to that darker side?

Art that really moves me and excites me is art that is pretty surreal and nightmarish — things that make you link into some other dream world. Art and theatre for me are not about realism. I find it exciting to have extremes, death and blood, things about extremities of life and living and dream states. Without being pretentious, that for me turns me on. I'm not interested about making work about people making a cup of tea. People being murdered and having bizarre sex, I find that more interesting to work with.

How much of your writing draws on Jewish folklore and Jewish history?

Some, to an extent. I've researched into Jewish folklore and I use a few Yiddish words in the

25

Amanda Moss in pre-Dragon Ladies days.
Mutant Wife Series, 1994.

Photo © Rupert Graves

piece. The style of the writing is very folklorish and fairy tale-ish. The show is an amalgamation of all the different things I was reading. I like old Jewish stories and Jewish traditional storytelling, but I don't know if there's any direct referencing to that in this particular show.

What is the distinction between you doing your regular stripping and doing the Dragon Ladies?

It's just so different you can't compare. When I'm stripping for money in the stripclub, I'm playing with one role — it's a very simple role that I play, and whilst I'm the author of my own dances and choose my own music and my own costumes, the reason I'm doing the performance is purely to get money from people for watching me dance, and for seeing my body. Whilst I'm interested in old strip styling and burlesque styling, and I try and camp it up a bit and do interesting stripteases, at the end of the day I only have one motive in that performance — which normally lasts about 10 minutes — and that is to take all my clothes off in an exciting and exotic manner and make as much money from people as I can! The Dragon Ladies work is *work* — it's not about money, though I'd obviously like to have better funding. It's my work, my imagination; complex images and collaboration with two really interesting artists. I could never do anything as complex or as interesting as that in a stripclub, because nobody would want to know. Stripping is a very basic form of performance. Although it's influenced the way I perform for myself, and given me a certain edge as a performer, I think of stripping as an art but *not my art*. It's not my complete picture.

Do you ever feel like subverting your regular stripshows, like dropping a bit of Dolly Blue in there?

The thing is I'm not there to give some kind of art morality show, I'm there to make money so I can go and do art on my own terms. I don't need to do it on [the punters'] terms. I'm there to make money, and if I start messing around... yeah, it might make some interesting art subversion, but I'd probably be out of a job. Just by having great big tattoos and dancing to really odd music kind of does that anyway.

What music do you dance to?

All manner of things from Fifties bump'n'grind through to Portishead. Indie noise to retro funny things. But nothing too obscure, otherwise people would walk away.

That raises an interesting question as to the importance of sound on a stripper's audience.

Absolutely.

• •

KATHARINE GIFFORD

Snowpony.
Singer and songwriter.

The line-up for Snowpony is pretty minimal. Is that a concerted effort?

When we first started we did experiment with

things like having someone play the loops live. It's just impossible actually, because of the way the timing goes. Lots of weird little arrangement things.

Who constructs the loops?
Me.

So do you play around with a song or come up with a loop first?
I kind of do both at the same time. I spend loads of time making loops and most of the time none of them get used. Lots of bits of songs that never get used either.

You're the main songwriter?
Yeah.

Why did you go separate ways with Stereolab?
I just left to do my own music. It was a band I joined knowing they already had two songwriters. I joined knowing that I wasn't going to be there forever.

Snowpony was recently described to me as an Indie supergroup. [*Deb on bass was also in My Bloody Valentine, Max the drummer was in Quick Space.*] Is that a bad tag?
It's bollocks.

What is your goal with Snowpony and how close are you to getting there?
About a million miles away. No, we can still go a long way musically, but I'm happy with the way its proceeding. It's a weird one, I wouldn't say I was pleased with the songs, but I think I've achieved what I wanted to with the earlier songs and now I'm moving onto different stuff, and it's working. Kind of.

Are you going to be changing the name of the band at some point?
Changing the name of the band? I wasn't planning on changing it.

Do you have an affinity with the
burlesque ethic?
Er… I'm not sure what the burlesque ethic is. I'm a 'show off' if that's what you mean.

● ● ● ● ● ● ● ● ● ● ● ● ● ● ● ● ● ● ●

JASON WILCOX

Film Show man.
Radical anthropologist.

How did you meet the Dragon Ladies?
There was a brief clip of one of their early shows on late-night TV last Summer, along with a short interview with Marisa. I was intrigued by what she was saying, and also by the name itself: 'Dragon Ladies' — I go to an evening class which is all about the *meaning* of dragons. Following that, I went to see their next show, in October of last year, which was at Oxton Hall, an old Victorian Music Hall near Hackney. I got in touch with them and interviewed them for a magazine called *Spirit*. I also encouraged them to go along to my evening class, as it was very near to their studio at the time. In the class I'm looking at the way stories are structured; magical stories, fairy tales, for example. The story they were doing for that show was the Bluebeard story, which fit in very well with what we were doing in our evening class.

So they all came along to the evening class?
Yes. The whole interest for me in their show is the way Marisa changes her identity. That's very important in the stories we look at. All magical stories are about transformation; characters turning from a human into a monster.

Marisa is very interested in music hall.
I think that comes out mostly at the beginning of the show, with the Dolly Blue character — the Victorian language ges-

what the Dragon Ladies have: there's sincerity in what they do, which makes it disturbing in a way. You can't just laugh it off, shrug it away. It's performed with a conviction.

There was a clip I showed from *Dracula*… the dragon is usually presented as a kind of demon, which has to be killed by the saints. But originally the dragon would have been — in our theory — an image of power, of good, connected to women and connected to pre-Christian times. And something like Dracula is connected to that. Vampires are a kind of animal-husband to the woman, and this goes into an elaborate theory of human origins and the origins of drama and ritual. I think they're subconsciously drawing on these notions in the Dragon Ladies…

The Dragon Ladies are not dealing with social realism — although there is a bit of that with the basic idea of a woman being threatened and maltreated by her husband. But the way it's actually developed takes you into far deeper areas of surrealism. It's very visual. You can't easily put it into words. You're in the audience looking at it. The emotional response in the films is similar. It's a poetic heightening of reality.

tures she uses there, and the imitating of the husband. But it's very black; not playing it like a straight music hall.

How did you choose the clips you did for the film show?

I was using the same basic plot development as the Dragon Ladies did in their show. I was also choosing the films for a visual reason. I tried with all of these films to show things that were made with a certain *sincerity*, because I think that's

The Dragon Ladies can be reached at:
Stanley House, St Chads Place, London, WC1X 9HH

Look out for Snowpony's debut album, *The Slow Motion World of Snowpony*, hopefully available by the time you read this.

TRAVELLING LIGHT
PORTLAND AND SEATTLE
December 1997

Jack Sargeant

Jack Sargeant outside Reading Frenzy. Photo © Marne Lucas

*Insanity. I spent much of Novem-
ber on the road, reading with Lydia
Lunch across Europe. After a few
days off in England I was flying to
New York to work for Creation
Books, and hang out for a week.
After that I flew to San Francisco,
where I spent eight or nine days
researching for my forthcoming
book. Because Marne Lucas knew I was going to be on the West Coast she
decided to compere a selection of readings and film screenings in Portland and
Seattle, with me appearing as her guest. So on December 17, I flew from San
Francisco to Portland with photographer and zinester Julie Peasley.*

*As ever this diary is collated from notes and memories, and with the invalu-
able assistance of both Marne Lucas and Julie Peasley.*

Wednesday 17th December

Julie has agreed to come to Portland. She's off work with carpal tunnel [syndrome] from
repetitive button-pressing in the photographic lab so she has nothing better to do but work
with me anyway. Sonny drives us to the BART, and we arrive in good time to catch the
subway to Oakland airport. As we climb from the car two disasters happen: firstly I realise
I've trodden in a massive dog turd and have stunk out the 4x4. More seriously, Julie has
forgotten her handbag, which contains her credit card and ID — a necessity if we want to
drink alcohol. Sonny and Julie race off, back to the warehouse where Sonny works to
collect her bag. It's not there, and they have to drive all the way back to the apartment in
Berkeley.

Our flight leaves in one hour.

I smoke a camel and wait.

And wait.

And wait.

It feels like ages, but is probably only 20 minutes, and then Julie appears. Somehow
she managed to get dropped off and walk past me into the BART, while I was outside. I see
her just before she gets on the train, and shout, "Lets grab a taxi". We're lucky and get one
straight away. Dive in and head for the airport. The cab driver decides to drive slowly. The
plane leaves in 20 minutes. I watch the clock ticking time, as we crawl along in rush hour
traffic. I can taste blood in my mouth from nervously biting my tongue. Eventually we get
to the airport. Julie slams her credit card on the counter, and books the two flights. One
return (hers) and my single (I'm heading back to the UK from Portland). The tickets are

printed out in slow-motion, in my name, a problem waiting to be discovered… but that's another story. She grabs them and we run for our departure gate, which is — of course — the furthest from the hall. We run onto the plane, the last two people to get on board. Julie doesn't like flying. I try and encourage her to look at the pink red splash of sun set but give up. We have a glass of wine. The flight only takes one hour then we're landing in Portland. We both have head colds. As we land our ears are meant to pop. Unfortunately Julie's don't, they just hurt. She can hardly hear.

Portland airport is a building site. Apparently several workers have been injured in accidents here. I can believe it. We leave the check-out building and have to stand in a queue under a massive tarpaulin shelter. Suddenly an old large thoroughly fucked looking bad-ass-American-muscle-car pulls up and Marne leaps out screaming "Jack!" Like a moment from some cheesy old film I drop everything and we embrace. I introduce Julie and we throw our bags in the back and climb in. Marne introduces us to our driver: Jacob Pander, comic book creator (Exquisite Corpse, Triple X) and her collaborator on the film The Operation. We cruise into town in style.

It's spitting rain and colder than SF. We dump our bags at Marne's apartment and meet her flatmate/sister Megan, then we head downtown to Berbati's, a fantastic Greek restaurant and bar. We eat squid, drink wine, and live like kings, while Marne and Jacob introduce us to what seems like everybody in town, including Jacob's brother and artistic collaborator Arnold.

Top **On the road with** (L–R) **Jack, Marne Lucas and Jacob Pander.**
Above **Jack, Julie Peasley and Sean Tejaratchi.**
Photos © Marne Lucas

After diner we head to Mary's. This is the coolest strip joint I've been too. Most American bars like this don't allow the girls to be completely naked — just topless, but not so in the glorious state of Oregon, which allows total nudity. The strippers are hot. One of them dances to Nick Cave's 'Red Right Hand', bumping and grinding to the song's heavy lurching rhythm. Sitting with Marne, Julie, Jacob and Arnold it's like I've died and gone to Heaven. What's even more strange is the strip club is decorated with a mural depicting Portland's working men which looks like it was painted by Tom of Finland.

2 AM. Julie and I now both have bad San Francisco colds. Marne makes us a health tea combination of garlic, ginger, lemon etc. Unfortunately she doesn't have all the ingredients, so we head for a 24-hour yuppie supermarket to buy them. Jacob and Marne don't drink, but both have had at least alcoholic beverage. Julie and I are shitfaced. Somebody in our party — who shall remain unnamed — manages to knock over a display of fruit,

sending grapefruits rolling across the highly-polished floor. I buy a litre of cranberry juice, which seems to help fight hangovers if you drink it before you go to bed.

Back at the apartment Marne makes the tea for us. We hang out till late/early.

Thursday 18th December

I have a show tonight, spoken word at a cool cafe called Umbra Penumbra. I'm reading with Beat celebrity, author of Mala Noche, and Gus Van Sant collaborator Walt Curtis. We spend the day sight-seeing and playing tourists, visiting various cafés, and hipster stores, including the excellent Reading Frenzy. This particular store is run by Chloe Eudaly — one of the sponsors of the

Jack and Rex Church.
Photo © Julie Peasley

film show — and specialises in selling cool literature, from underground zines to bizarre books. Sean Tejaratchi from Crap Hound — the clip art zine — works there, and proves to be a great guy. I spend a small fortune on things that I tell myself are necessary research materials. Over coffee in Umbra Penumbra I get to meet Rex Church, local Church of Satan representative and underground artist, who paints gloriously dark apocalyptic visions of Hell.

Chloe is selling my books at the events and has managed to get hold of everything I ever wrote or contributed to. Which is pretty disturbing. I promise everybody dinner, and we head for a local Japanese restaurant. Here we discover the delights of the sushi train, which races around the massive counter, as the customers grab plates of food from it. I seem to be totally disabled by the experience, every time the train comes close I ask Chloe which one's vegetarian, by the time she's told me it has gone past so I have to wait for it to come around again. Somehow I manage to eat something. Then I realise I only have $30 and the bill is pushing $50. I ask Julie to lend me some — luckily she has a few dollars left. We make the bill, and head to the reading.

Unbelievably there is a crowd at the reading, Marne has done an incredible job and it seems that all of Portland's underground scenesters are there. I get to talk to Rex, and mortician and performer Gerry. Walt's reading is full of life and Beat positivity. He's wired on alcohol and rips for an hour. Then I get on stage. Audience/performer relationships are hard to maintain, and — just as he made everybody feel good, I make them feel bad, spitting bitterly humorous short stories one after another. About 20 people 'get it' but many more look terrified/pissed off/leave. Fuck 'em. Jacob videos the event, capturing my mixture of alcoholic narcolepsy and vitriol for posterity.

Marne, Julie, Jacob and I head back to Berbati's for drinks. People keep buying them. I keep drinking them. At some point the four of us go to a late-night Italian restaurant.

Much later we go back to Marne's apartment and watch some short films by local filmmaker Vanessa Renwick.

Julie is still deaf, although her ears are beginning to pop now.

Late to bed, again.

Friday 19th December

Julie's cold is nearly gone when she wakes up. My cold hasn't gone, but I'm an early riser

Jack doing his spoken word thing at the Umbra Penumbra cafe. Photo © Marne Lucas

and I've been standing on the porch of the apartment smoking cigarettes since 8 AM. I make coffee. Marne wakes up. She has a sore throat. I kind of feel guilty for bringing the SF cold with me. We drink coffee then jump in a cab to go to the local radio station, to do an interview for the evening's Deathtripping Film Show, at the Film Centre. Following the interview we go for breakfast, walking downtown, through Portland, which is — it should be said — a great city to walk in.

Today is a very special day. Marne has managed to get Julie and me into the morgue of one of the major hospitals. I am so excited I can hardly contain myself. Breakfast can't go by fast enough. Then it's time to visit the dead. The three of us meet our gracious host Gerry in the canteen, his partner, Casandra, has come along too. Excitedly we head to the morgue. The morgue is in the basement of the building, painted pus yellow, a white board hangs on one wall describing the state of various organs found in bodies during autopsy. The autopsy table is clean, and the air smells of detergent.

Gerry picks up a bone saw — the show has begun — and turns it on, the high buzz and whine filling the strangely reverent silence of the room. Turning he pulls it down onto Casandra's arm… nothing happens, no shower of blood or scream. Then he brings the saw down onto a cardboard tissue box which vanishes beneath a grey-spray of grinding cardboard. The saw can only cut through certain textures and living flesh is not one of them. Next, Gerry walks to the refrigerator and opens it. In true carny showman style he pulls out a cardboard box, stained brown with blood splatter across its surface. "I don't even know what's in here!" He tells us, as we lean forward, the familiar taste of anticipation and fear in our mouths. He unwraps the first bundle, it's two dismembered human hands, frozen clutching each other. He pulls them apart, ice flicks across us from the yellow and brown flesh stumps. Opening another packet from the box we see that it too contains human hands. Gerry and Casandra explain the musculature of the meat, which resembles beef in texture and colour, while Julie and Marne snap photos and we all ask questions. Then Gerry lets us peek into the ice box, which is stacked with neat rows of red bags, each of which contains a gangrenous human leg.

Next he takes us to the store room. Unlike the ultra clean morgue this room is used for storing all the various pieces of meat waiting for disposal, or being kept for research. The air is thick with the smell of formaldehyde, which makes us feel slightly sick (it is also a carcinogen, but hey, we wanted fun). The shelves are lined with blood and chemical splattered boxes, and glass jars full of brains/livers/lungs/pancreas etc., however the high point is a large plastic tub. "What's this?" one of us asks, pointing at the filthy yellow butter jelly. Gerry smiles and states "Oh. That's just some liposuction fat taken off some woman's ass and thighs". Wow. We leave our tour feeling more than satisfied. Outside the hospital Jacob picks us up in the car and we cruise back to Marne's for coffee.

Marne and Jacob head over to the Film Centre for the evening's show, which Marne is curating. Julie and I head to Umbra Penumbra to hook up with Jim Goad and Sky Ryan for coffee. Julie telephones her pen pal Jerry Blue, who agrees to come and meet us. After a brief coffee Jim and Sky head off.

Julie, Jerry and I head for the screening via a massive mall. In the mall we see a group of women. In underwear. Agreeing that it must be the worst job on the planet we approach the living models and ask if we can be photographed with them. They agree. It should be noted that Jerry is something of an expert on employment in Portland, having been fired from every major company — and a lot of minor ones as well — in the city. He specialises in hustling, and surviving by his wits. In a country with such minimal welfare provision I am very impressed, and — unaware of his capacity for consumption — vow to buy him drinks all night.

At the Film Centre I have to organise all the videos and talk to the staff, and help Chloe set up the books for any customers. I haven't eaten, and feel very hungry. Plus my cold is really beginning to kick in bad. Julie and Jerry vanish in search of food, which they find literally minutes before I get on stage to introduce the films. I stand there giving a lecture while eating very-cheap-but-filling Mexican food. Yum.

Signing books afterwards one guy comes up to me and asks about Simon — Rapid Eye — Dwyer, I tell him about Simon's death, and — like so many people — he tells me what an important influence Rapid Eye was on him.

Exhausted, Marne and Jacob head off. Julie, Jerry, two guys whose names escape me, and myself all head back to Berbati's which appears to have become our regular drinking haunt. Here Jerry reveals his talent for telling some of the most obnoxious racist and sexist jokes I have ever heard. A lot of beer is consumed. At some point I switch to vodka, Julie to Midouri Sours, and Jerry to bourbon. Jerry's jokes continue for hours as he routinely annihilates the ethnic background, sexuality, and moral laxity of everybody in the bar. Soon the barmaid joins in too. For a misanthrope he sure is popular. At some point, somehow, we find ourselves in the cool local 24-hour porno store, and Kenkos to collect some prints (what a culture 24-hour porno *and* 24-hour photo developing). Then we are driven back to Marne's apartment. Julie and I talk and make plans until near-dawn, before falling into uneasy drunken/exhilarated sleep for three hours.

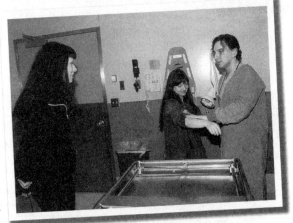

Top **Descent to the morgue.** L–R **Gerry, Casandra, Marne, Julie, Jack.** Photo © Marne Lucas
Above **Demonstrating the bone saw. Marne, Casandra and Gerry.** Photo © Julie Peasley

Saturday 20th December

I feel sick. Marne now has a really bad cold and has all but lost her voice. Julie is heading back to San Francisco today, while I'm heading the opposite way to Seattle. We hang out for the morning. Julie telephones Jerry and they agree to meet for breakfast. I hate goodbyes. Walk Julie to the bus stop. Perfunctory hug. Miserable. Wave good-bye. Back to apartment, stand outside and smoke.

Jacob arrives. Time to leave. We pack the car and drive out of Portland, stopping on the way to buy chocolate and crisps. I find a tee-shirt in the store that reads: OREGON THE BEAVER STATE and have to buy it. We hit the interstate. The countryside is incredibly beautiful. I become aware of exactly how big America is. Portland and Seattle are virtually next to each other, yet are some 400 miles apart, with little in-between except mountains and woodland.

Marne falls into sickly sleep in the back of the car, Jacob and I talk. About 70 miles out of Portland the car begins to smell odd. Smoke starts to come from under the hood. We pull over — Marne sleeps on — and Jacob checks the engine, which looks fine. We drive on. Jacob tells me he has no AAA (in other words: if we break down we don't have anybody who will pick us up and drive us to a mechanic), but that the whole thing should be fine. Ten miles down the road, and the car is rapidly filling up with grey blue smoke, which is, by now, billowing from under the hood. Jacob pulls over, the front wheels hit a ditch and the car tips savagely, throwing the still-sleeping Marne onto the floor. Startled, she wakes, shouting "What's wrong?" All Jacob and I can do is laugh. I try and explain that the car appears to have been on fire, while he goes off for help.

Only a couple of weeks back Lydia Lunch told me that the Pacific coast of the USA is "the serial killer corridor", because there are more murderers loose here than anywhere else. I also start remembering that we are in Big Foot country. And — possibly more realistically — bear country. In the middle of nowhere. Shit.

Jacob returns with directions (from whom?) to a small town with a garage, we drive there, windows open, the whole car stinking of melting-camembert-shit. Ten miles. We nearly choke. At the garage they cut some old piece of the now-redundant air conditioning fan from inside the engine... free of charge, everything okay. We hit the road. I fall asleep.

Seattle: Thai food. Book signing okay. The dapper Joel Bacher has organised the show at the Speakeasy Cafe. I screen a couple of Beat movies, answer questions, cough, but smoke regardless. Joel's partner Bette lets us all sleep in her magnificent apartment. It is huge. I sleep like a baby.

Sunday 21st December

Marne can barely talk. Her glands are swollen. She looks like she may die. My cold is rough but stable. Jacob is clearly indestructible. We hang out, Bette and Joel make us an incredible Middle Eastern style omelette and we drink coffee and juice before hitting the road again.

Sunlight over Seattle is beautiful. As we drive out of town Jacob flicks the radio on, and blasts Hendrix's 'Hey Joe' through the car. Marne sleeps again. The road is good and we hit Portland by dusk.

There's a Winter Solstice Party at Umbra Penumbra. Dancer and artist Kitty Diggins performs a sexy pagan light ceremonial dance. Jerry Blue turns up, we drink beers. I also get to meet comic book artist Joe Stacco. So much to say, but there's never enough time.

Get to bed at, maybe, 4:00 AM.

Monday 22nd December

5:30 AM. Jacob wakes me... drives me to the airport. Here I drink copious quantities of coffee. In 24 hours I'll be back in England. 🌀

Jack Sargeant is author of *Deathtripping: The Cinema of Transgression* and *Naked Lens: Beat Cinema*. Volume one of his forthcoming book on underground art, *Suture*, will be published by Creation Books in August 1998.

PAM & TOMMY LEE
Hardcore & Uncensored
Starring: PAMELA ANDERSON LEE, TOMMY LEE
Directed by: PAMELA ANDERSON LEE, TOMMY LEE
AN IEG PRESENTATION, US, 1998. 70 MINUTES

Howard Lake

Here it is at last, the one every Saturday afternoon mutton-flogger has been waiting for. Having been peddled online the world over for almost a year, 'that' home movie finally receives a quasi-legit release[1], giving devotees of Überbimbo Pamela Anderson Lee intimate — often *very* intimate — access to their fantasy-object's private life. As tapes walk out of US stores, in the UK this low-budget verité production should have appeared in a dodgy boozer near you as we speak. I'd recommend you rush to dupe one, or run the risk of missing something quite extraordinary.

For readers not up to speed yet, the story goes something like this: siliconised saucepot Anderson weds tattooed rock 'wild man' Tommy Lee, drummer with iffy metallists Motley Crüe.[2] Subsequently, the infatuated couple set up house, pursue their careers, hang out with pals, go on vacation and indulge in as much sex as you'd expect from a pair of newly-weds. So far, so normal — except that they decided to keep a video record of these first few months of marriage, from the service itself to the consummation and beyond. Of course, it's this tape which, having been lifted from the Lee household by persons unknown, is now doing the rounds of unashamed voyeurs and Schadenfreude freaks everywhere.

Just how and under what exact circumstances the tape became a commercial product remains mired in confusion. The company behind the release, Internet Entertainment Group, are a shadowy combine, perhaps with links to sexvid producers Vivid Video. Their website divulges next to nothing on either how they acquired the tape or what deal was struck to release it. They claim a legal agreement prevents their talking details but that hasn't stemmed a barrage of rumours both on the web and in print media, some of which name names of those alleged to have done the pilfering and even circulate claims that Pam and Tommy intended their movie to gain a greater audience. The latter must be treated with scepticism, to say the least. But what of the grubby little memento itself?

IEG have chosen to use title cards to establish continuity and narrative —'Pre-Nuptials', 'The Day After', 'Going On Vacation' and so on. This simple device is surprisingly effective, imposing as it does a kind of documentary structure on the raw footage. Presented in this manner, the film

PAMELA ANDERSON

"DON'T CALL ME BABE!"

BARB·WIRE

From the Producers of "The Mask"

PolyGram

resembles a BBC2 Video Diary, albeit with far more fascinating subjects than TV's standard twat-with-a-camcorder.

Here, the twat with a camcorder is Pammy, owner of one of the most cherished glory-boxes of the Nineties. Quite why such an honour should fall to her specifically has always bemused me, as there seems to be no discernible difference between Ms Lee and any number of sun-bleached beach bunnies cluttering the California coastline. Her acting can often border on the risible, her screen presence and charisma are nil and she shows an aptitude for thesping so basic you can virtually see the wheels going round. Physically — always a vexed and subjective area — her principal asset appears to constitute nothing more than that her physiognomy conforms to consensus definitions of sexual allure: hips, lips, tits and a tousled blonde mane. As dream factory blondes go, Pammy's a pale imitation of those in whose stilettos she obviously means to totter. There's no Monroe-esque vulnerability, none of the va-voom of Mansfield or the mystique of Bardot. Sure, her screen persona attempts to incorporate her antecedents' character traits, but as so often happens when one attempts to construct by committee, the end product possesses a homogenised blandness all image and zero substance. Which is as neat a metaphor for late 20th Century mass culture as any, but still fails to adequately explain why 8 out of 10 pubescent boys prefer to starch their sheets to an image of Pam than any other purveyor of pre-packaged pulchritude. It also justifies your reviewer indulging in a shameless bout of voyeurism in the name of research…

Writing in **Crackpot** of a visit to LA's Muscle Beach, John Waters noted: "Intently watching another voyeur as he voyeurs an exhibitionist is a thrill you probably won't get at home." Now, for $19.95, you can. These snatched 70 minutes offer a detailed analysis of two narcissists deeply in love with each other and with the third party in their life: the camcorder. The portrait etched out of the jumbled, often confused frames is of an intense, almost desperate passion acted out in a series of vignettes which move between being variously mundane to explicitly graphic to the sometime surreal.

Pam herself comes across pretty much as you expected. She's no polymath, that's for certain, but then who expected her to be lounging naked in the Jacuzzi reading Schopenhauer? Based on the evidence of **Hardcore & Uncensored** Pammy exhibits a certain child-like wonder at her world coupled with a fair degree of sexual adventure and uninhibition. Whether this is due to judicious editing on the part of the producers eager to give punters as sexualised a study of Pammy as possible remains moot. Out-takes may well show a hard-nosed, ruthless and scheming careerist under the peroxide, but somehow we'd doubt it. Then again, one has to remember that her emotional state when these scenes were filmed. Even the most rigorous cynic cannot deny that she is totally, utterly drunk on the glorious passion that exists between herself and her Tommy, the man she is convinced is the love of her life.

Hindsight's a wonderful and often cruel thing. At time of writing, the **National Enquirer** (17/3/98) is hyperventilating on tales of beatings, devil worship and marital contracts signed in blood, plus teasers for even more outlandish revelations concerning Pammy's tribulations at Tommy's hands: "'Tommy called me a whore and a slut and every rotten name he could think of,' the blonde beauty confided to an insider." This is a far cry from the reportage of 1995, the year this footage was shot, when, between endlessly extolling her spouse's prodigious endowment, our heroine traded tales of a sensual idyll where Tommy played piano while Pammy hovered above him naked on a swing (and, believe it or not, the very swing makes an appearance here — unoccupied, mind). Between then and now, there's been motherhood, the critical derision that greeted **Barb Wire** and rumoured overdoses, suicide attempts and much much more for the tabloids and their slavering readers to savour. They who live by the media shall surely die by the media — so take heed when Pam starts comparing herself to Our Lady of the Alma Bridge.[3]

Wiser heads might have anticipated the outcome and rendered hindsight irrelevant. Who can forget the bizarre cir-

cumstances of the courtship, which involved, among other things, Tommy purchasing a $1000's worth of sex toys, a five-day romance in Cancun and a beach wedding 12 hours after their first date… all of which the happy couple — and publicists — were delighted to share with a media which gleefully lapped up such a celebrity ready-made and instigated a 24-hour stakeout by way of response, counting the days until the whole rickety edifice collapsed.

And collapse it would, they could be sure of that — in media eyes it had to, for both parties conform so rigorously to their respective stereotypes of bosomy starlet and deranged rock monster as to be virtual cartoon representations. Tommy's stormy relationship with Heather Locklear, another airbrushed TV blonde, provided an identikit script for the media to follow; Pammy's trail of discarded suitors — among them such tabloid dreamboats as Dean 'Superman' Cain, WWF star Shawn 'Heartbreak Kid' Michaels and Scott 'Chachi from **Happy Days**' Baio — demonstrated a capricious and fickle nature (plus a trailer park aesthetic where men were concerned) at odds with the right stuff of contented wedlock. And, not so much lurking in the wings but centre stage and lapping up the applause, was more SEX than a newsroom sub could shake a stick at.

Pammy and Tommy are a special case, a hypersexualised dream team — renowned superstud and carnal dynamo; a tabloid fantasy comparable to, say, Marilyn Monroe and John C. Holmes getting it on. That two such fantasy-defined figures should conjoin and then broadcast the details of their couplings left tabloid heads spinning with lubricious intoxication. It was too much, much too much and, as any media-savant knows, anyone who's getting it that good *must* be made to pay.

Tertiary sexual issues also came to the fore. If only Pam didn't insist on babbling on about Tommy's tallywhacker! For all her supposed artfulness at playing the media game it never occurred to her that to a lot of men — male journos especially — size really *does* matter. Bad enough Tommy Lee was nailing their quintessential piece of ass day and night; that he excelled in it too only rubbed salt in the wounds. Males might harbour anything from veiled admiration to resentful envy toward their oversized peers, but such ire is nothing compared to the opprobrium they reserve for females who proclaim that, yes, bigger is better and biggest is best. Macho equilibrium must be restored and thus, logic inverted, it is the woman's character which must be at fault in some way. Adolescent schoolyard smut theory: she needs a jumbo jamoke because *she*

Many porn magazines employ a legal team who dissect and analyse each issue before it goes to press. The above excerpts are taken from a letter from one such legal team, advising its client against using certain 'sensitive' (!) Pamela Anderson references in an article scheduled for their up-coming edition.

is oversexed, maybe had too *much* sex, slept around, is literally a 'loose woman'.[4] Dumb sexist logic, to be sure, but remember the ledger of Pam's past lovers, the 'roadkill to the altar' in a classic piece of Enquirer-speak.[5] The subtext is only just concealed, but quickly becomes evident as the catalogue of conquests, helpfully annotated just in case, moves from one industry mover and shaker to another, up to and including the archetypal Hollywood Mr Big, then-powerful producer Jon Peters. The implication is clear: the female ascent of the Mount Showbiz invariably involves sexual favours. As it was for the original dream blonde Monroe, so it must also be for this decade's model. Except, unlike Marilyn, Pam didn't make it in Tinseltown and then declare: "That's the last cock I ever suck."

She most certainly did not and, if proof be needed, Hardcore & Uncensored sure delivers, with several shaky close-ups of those legendary lips stretched around Tommy's unit. These scenes are verification of a globalised fantasy, a vivid actualisation of the unified desires of millions of males who have co-opted, almost by media osmosis, the idea of this face and this figure as their ultimate erotic fulfilment. As Tom Wolfe wrote in his essay The Shockkkkkk of Recognition[6], there is almost a transcendental moment when a star or celebrity is seen outside of their accepted milieu, when they are caught by a camera lens in a way that they, for a rare moment, cannot control. A transference of power takes place and we mere mortals are no longer in obeisance to their status. Hype, PR and the entire apparatus which fabricates and maintains celebrity count for nothing once we have them — on our terms not theirs. Wolfe was writing about a hobby paparazzo seeking to capture the image of Natalie Wood, but identical strictures apply to Hardcore & Uncensored, only in this instance the degree of ingress into forbidden realms is many times advanced from a sneaked snapshot outside a restaurant or hotel. The degree of shock is amplified a hundredfold, to the finite point of media-manipulated desire.

    The fan/fantasist fixated on a sexual wish never to be attained now comes so close as almost makes no difference. OK, it's not *his* dick getting blown on that screen, but now he no longer has need to imagine Pamela Anderson performing sexually, he has achieved a form of consummation-by-proxy via that purloined tape. The more he studies those crucial frames, the better acquainted he becomes with the sexual habits of his devotional object. For example, he now knows Pammy's idea of fun is to go down on her man while driving down an Interstate; he knows also she doesn't like to swallow, or even that, her admiration of meatpackers aside, she can require extra lube to accommodate such an appendage. These kind of intimate details, he knows, are properly only the knowledge of a lover (indeed, even I feel squeamish writing them here), but by the time you read this millions of men the world over will also possess that knowledge. Furthermore, by the very circumstances in which the film came to be made, they will feel they have established a definitive understanding of her sexual traits. These scenes are not dictated by script, director or stylist. The sexuality on show is nothing like the manicured and arch eroticism of Baywatch, Barb Wire or even the numerous nude images posed for Playboy, or the poster hanging on the fan's bedroom wall. He no longer engages with her image in the removed fashion to which he was accustomed, the image a simulacrum of eroticism or a performed sexuality intended to be shared by millions. It's now just me and you, Pammy, me and you.

As mentioned previously, these scenes depict a relationship marked by an intense desire. Anyone who may have dismissed Anderson's unabashed vaunting of Tommy's tadger will soon accept she was telling no lies — either regarding his dimensions or her admiration of it. Control of the camera switches between husband and wife throughout, but about 70% of the scenes we see are filmed by Pam. Selective editing again, certainly, but one can't help but concede that she is overwhelmed with affection both for 'it' and its owner. With Pam behind the camera we therefore become extremely well-acquainted with the pair of them over the course of the tape's run time, as even the most banal sequence will feature yet another demand for Tommy to 'whip it out'. On occasion, even he seems reluctant, as though being asked to perform his party piece one time too many, but those moments are few and far between as we've realised right from the start that Tommy's not the world's most retiring guy. It's plain he revels in his celebrity and — perhaps more than his wife — understands what a sublime couple they make. Via his and, subsequently, her recording the intimate minutiae of their lives they pay tacit homage to the force which brought them together. Without the status confirmed upon them by the media it's probable they would never have met; they would have remained small-town nobodies with big dreams. That's a feeling you sense both feel, and perhaps that's why the camera played such a profound role during this time. At one point Pammy hints the recordings are being made for their kids — she's extolling the glories of Tommy's lingam at the time — but the viewer's impression is more of a couple whose identities are wholly interpreted through the lens, who are almost devoid of character or meaning without a need to perform, however limited their audience.

There's little doubt all of us perform to some degree during sex, whether for our partner's benefit or our own gratification. How we learn the way to act relies upon our experiences, environment and the archetypes in which we are versed. In the Nineties it is virtually a certainty that the protocols of pornography will encroach upon boudoir behaviour. All of us, smut-addicts or not, are drilled in the erotic. Any child old enough to read a tabloid can discern the accepted form of congress, the words and phrases used at the height of passion. As one reaches adulthood the etiquette changes according to predilection and inhibition. One can expand erotic input to include hardcore porn and take cues from the conventions of that particular genre.

This is worth mentioning as the immediate thought that hits the observer when Pam and Tommy finally get down to business is how acutely it resembles production-line porn. Were you, without knowing the participants' identities, to see a few frames intercut with generic modern hardcore you'd be forgiven for guessing it to be the work of any one of the numerous Buttman manqués grinding out shagnasty tapes in the States these days, auteurs like Ed Powers, Max Hardcore and Rodney Moore, to name but three. The manner in which the Lees filmed each other indicates an understanding of how hardcore operates. This is no better illustrated than in the episode where Tommy and Pam are off on vacation — a scene that has eerie echoes of Fingered's Marty Nations/Lydia Lunch two-hander — and Pam goes down on Tommy as he's at the wheel. When collagen meets cock, Tommy's porno instinct cuts in. "'Move your hair so you can see!'" he babbles, pushing Pam's locks aside so as not to obscure the recording of his penis

notes

1. For which the protagonists reportedly — at time of writing — stood to gain around $80m in royalties.

2. Seems Crüe members make a habit of this kind of thing — IEG had a release scheduled for April '98 of another privately shot tape featuring singer Vince Neal in three-way action with porn performer Janine Lindemuller. This one should do good business as Janine's X-rated USP is that she only does all-girl scenes in her movies, something that's irked smut hounds for years.

3. And, yet again, there's synergy in that there VT — just as the Saintly One's last moments were frozen in time by the Ritz security cameras, so the timely appearance of *Hardcore & Uncensored* provides 'unauthorised' media access to a marriage we know failed. As the images of Diana passing through the hotel lobby are inextricably connected to images of the crumpled Mercedes, so the Lees' besotted abandon portrayed on tape presages the *Enquirer* shots of Pam's bruised and battered face.

4. There's an uncanny resonance here with racial sex myths in which the Negro male and his huge organ symbolise the last resort of the morally bankrupt female. Even today, the white woman who seeks black male lovers is often disdained by the males of her race and considered to be somehow sexually brainwashed. In the most ancestral memories, big dicks are invariably associated with perfidy and immorality — for a far older example consult Ezekiel, Ch. 23, the *Two Adulterous Sisters*, in your Bible.

5. Headline to a March story on Sharon Stone's latest wedding. In Hollywood, no one's slate is ever wiped clean.

6. Tom Wolfe, *The Pump House Gang*, Bantam 1968

7. In a moment of supreme irony, Tommy breaks off from a guided tour of their love nest to point out just such a video crew camped out on a hill overlooking their property.

between her lips, an act starkly reminiscent of blow job loops since time immemorial. Tommy knows, as all good pornographers know, that visibility is all. This trait is maintained throughout the other sex scenes and crowned with a by-the-numbers cum shot, Pam wiggling gleefully — but holding the shot — as her true love unloads over her million dollar bod.

How Pam and Tommy fuck off-camera is unknown, but with that third party present both appear galvanised into mimicking established porno customs. Much of their existence together, in fact, echoes the scripting of a standard fuck-flick: exaggerated phallic worship; the lovers grunting coarsely-phrased sweet nothings at each other; the constant needling arousal. The strangeness of it all can't be underplayed. Whereas many hardcore performers lead comparatively virtuous lives when not working, Tommy and Pammy — known to the world as the most sexualised couple there is — seem to be overcompensating in their private lives, as if showing to their camera that which they realise the world *really* wants from them; self-reflexivity gone berserk to such an extent the media fantasy imposed upon the celebrities becomes an actual, fully realised truth.

For our protagonists the future appears uncertain. For, as viewers absorbed in media systems and the voyeuristic culture this entails, we can only wonder as to **Hardcore & Uncensored**'s meaning. Media posits itself as the gateway to truth, yet only a fool would accept such a patent falsehood as gospel; we all understand media conventions, be they press, television or cinema, and recognise the levels of manipulation inherent in these processes. Our interaction with our media environment is predicated upon the extent of our understanding, but this tape seems to rewrite the rules of engagement. The success or otherwise of any media product ultimately rests upon the persons producing it — critical acclaim is irrelevant in a world where the bottom line is always financial. The USP (Unique Selling Point) with which this product is being sold to us is that it, in some way, constitutes a 'victory' for those of us — us sad bastards who merely watch and absorb — over the big bad Hollywood hype machine. But the bottom line must be that IEG are raking in the dollars by exploiting our desire to witness the private moments of media-created icons. Simultaneously the image is being both destroyed and reinforced, a paradox which almost defies analysis but which must constitute one of the most heightened convergences of media criteria thus far. Modern TV airtime is now crammed with shows offering 'intimate access' to stars' secrets, to the minutiae of their stellar lives. Video paparazzi stalk Beverly Hills and any other celebrity locales looking to steal unguarded, unstyled moments of these coveted existences[7], yet the same channels that broadcast such footage also air any amount of carefully-packaged, zealously-controlled programmes centred on the manicured image. What **Hardcore & Uncensored** reveals is that celebrity saturation has led to us making new demands upon the medium. As our understanding of the process increases so our requirements alter. We no longer want the image, we want the essence — the *reality*. **Candid Camera** becomes **Caught On Camera**; **Believe It Or Not** becomes **Real TV**; **Starsky & Hutch** becomes **World's Scariest Police Shoot-outs**…

And **Lifestyles Of The Rich And Famous** becomes **Pam & Tommy Lee: Hardcore & Uncensored**. At long last we get payback: the hype machine to which we are all in thrall gives up a flesh sacrifice to last us an eternity. ◉

weird weekends with Louis Theroux

David Kerekes

I n the opening months of 1998, BBC2 aired Louis Theroux's Weird Weekends, a series of four programmes devoted to exploring specific aspects of US fringe culture. The series arrived without much of a fanfare. But, intrigued by the promise of televangelists and religious cults, with no expectations whatsoever, this viewer tuned in to catch the first episode. Was he pleasantly surprised! Weird Weekends was funny, surreal, poignant, and chock full of misguided fanatics on a mission from a higher being. Most important, however, was the intrepid, bespectacled young fellow who held it all together: Louis Theroux. He passed no judgement on the craziness around him, hell, he even joined in without making a meal of it.

Come the following Thursday, I was tuned in again. This time Louis was off investigating UFO devotees, some of whom had psychic energy rifles with which they could immobilise alien invaders. Another devotee sat in a chair and, for a small fee, could channel the strange language — and even stranger messages — of a friendly space being.

Episode three was down to earth with a bang. Here Louis got embroiled in the porno business, got himself an agent and started volunteering nude snaps of himself to all and sundry. He made friends with a Godzilla-loving young stud, visited the Elegant Angel offices, and landed himself a walk-on part in a gay porn shoot.

For the final Weird Weekends, it was survivalists and far right militias, the Green Beret who had inspired Rambo, and a former computer whizkid who left it all behind for a life in a giant haystack.

An eye on fringe culture is not a new concept for television. Many presenters have been down similar paths to Weird Weekends before. Few, however, have felt comfortable enough to travel as light as Theroux does, or go without the support of a haughty or smug commentary. If Louis Theroux has a peer in television reportage, it must be the original globetrotter himself, Alan Whicker. Theroux shares that same laid-back, don't mind me approach. He ingratiates himself with most — not all — of the people he meets, and often jokes along with them. Sometimes, however, he doesn't let the joke go. Who can forget such classic Weird Weekends moments as Louis running through a script with porn actor Troy, and chiding him for not putting enough feeling into the line "I love you", insisting that he try it over and

41

over again (with each attempt sounding exactly as insipid as the last)? Or the conversation with the neo-Nazi in the bell-tower, who Louis coaxes to repeat "I'm free!" in the manner of camp Mr Humphries from the old British sitcom *Are You Being Served?*, alas without success?

It was literally days after the last episode of *Weird Weekends* aired in February that the opportunity to do an interview with Louis came about. Quite by chance, too.

HEADPRESS **What did Louis Theroux do prior to _Weird Weekends_?**

Art © Dogger

LOUIS I left college in 1991. Moved to America. Worked as a journalist in San Jose, California. Then got hired at *Spy* magazine, a New York satirical monthly. *Spy* folded at the beginning of 1994. Some friends at *Spy* had a connection with Michael Moore — of *Roger & Me* fame — and I got hired as a writer and correspondent on his show, *TV Nation*, right when it was just starting. It was a fluke, really. I got hired to do a segment on millennial groups, getting specifics on exactly when and how the world was going to end. I was the third choice for the position after the performance artist Karen Finley and the comedian Merrill Markoe. And that's only the people I know about! Anyway, after that, I sort of became *TV Nation's* designated Kooks Correspondent. I did segments on the Ku Klux Klan, Avon ladies in the Amazon, Ted Nugent, and others.

How did _Weird Weekends_ come about?
After *TV Nation* ended, the BBC signed me to a six-month development deal. *Weird Weekends* was one of the ideas I came up with. I was basically trying to come up with a format that would allow us to use many of the weird small moments of humour that would end up on the cutting room floor at *TV Nation*; and that would go beyond taking piss out of people on the fringe and acknowledge that in some ways these people are worthy of respect.

Am I right in saying that four episodes of the series have been televised? Are there any more, or do you intend to do more?
Four have gone out, which is all we've completed. We shot a Christmas special which will go out this Christmas. We're editing that at the moment. It involved bringing four of my favourite characters from the first series to New York for Christmas to see how we all got along. So you've got a porn performer, a fundamentalist, a UFO contactee and a survivalist, all getting on each other's nerves. Now we're in the early stages of doing another four *Weird Weekends*.

How would you set up one of your _Weekends_? How would you approach your subjects?
Each episode had its own producer/director and associate producer. We'd all pitch in during the research phase. Get names and contacts from papers, magazines, web sites, friends of friends. Then the producer and director would go out on a 10-day scout, shoot tape of some of the characters they encountered. We'd all sit down and plan the shoot around the characters we liked best, map out a rough story outline, dredge up more characters if we thought we needed them. We'd also come across new characters during the shoot proper, and drop other ones. The key is flexibility, adapting as you go.

How much sway does the phrase "BBC film crew" actually have in America?

The BBC is known and respected among Americans. The militia types in Idaho tended to regard us as less suspect than the US networks. The fundamentalists in Dallas tended to regard us as more suspect. To the others, I suppose we were like any TV outfit.

During the time you spent with the evangelical Christian groups in the first episode, it was clear that your approach was going to be different. You participated in activities without being cynical. It's kind of a 'naïve' approach, in a way.
I concentrate on being natural and not judging. I find it very refreshing to be around people with unorthodox beliefs. That's just who I am. It's not really cultivated.

Did you feel that the presence of the camera helped to open up your subjects?
I think many of them did feel they had a perspective they wanted to share with the world — about UFOs or Christianity or whatever — and they were grateful I was letting them do that.

Did you ever find yourself getting emotionally involved with the issues you were investigating?
I think you can see me getting emotionally involved on the show. I felt very bad for Mike Cain, the "radical noodle" in the Idaho show who seemed bent on having a showdown with the federal government. I was genuinely bummed out by the sleaziness of the Rob Black shoot in the Porn show. I think you have to allow yourself to be influenced up to a point, because that's what it is to be human, and to be an effective correspondent in this type of show, you have to react in a human way, otherwise you lose the audience.

Top Rob Black.
Above Mike Cain.

In the Porn programme, you mentioned that you couldn't do a couple of things that were put to you because the BBC wouldn't be happy. What kind of restrictions were put on your actions?
Actually, all in all, the BBC has been very supportive. Where we decided not to do certain things — like see me actually getting it on in a porn film — it was a creative decision, not something that was imposed on us. The only thing they were a bit funny about was showing me having too much fun with guns, because this was right after Dunblane. I think it was okay for me to shoot guns but I couldn't go "Woohoo! This is wicked!" But I didn't get the urge to say that anyway, so it was fine.

In a way, I suppose that the Porn episode was the least 'weird', as it's based around a commercial enterprise and the people in it are driven by money...
That's a debatable point. I know what you mean, but then, there are so many ways to earn money. If you look at someone like JJ Michaels — the young performer who plays with the Godzilla toys — he has a whole host of "weird" motivations that make him do what he does. I don't know that the decision to be in porno movies — with everything that that entails: alienating your family; risking AIDS, VD, etc. — is any less weird than, say, going out and trying to make contact with UFOs.

The Porn episode also showed the only instant where you seemed to get upset. (It happens on the Elegant Angel shoot for a sex film with an 'abduction' theme.) Do you think people like Elegant Angel are being mavericks in what is now a conveyor-belt industry, or are they just irresponsible?

43

"I <u>love</u> you." Louis helps Troy (left) with his dialogue.

I suppose it's both. I do think there's a way of being a maverick without degrading people the way [director] Rob Black does.

On several instances, you discover a seemingly contentious point with an interview subject and doggedly pursue it. In the Porn episode it happens twice with the same guy — Troy, the 'straight' porn star who claims only to do gay movies for the money. (He kinda reminded me of the Frank Zappa song 'Bobby Brown'.) Have you ever pushed any of your subjects 'too far'?

I've never been punched, if that's what you mean. I usually have pretty good antennae for when someone's going to snap. That moment with Troy is deceptive. We'd spent two days with him and he and I had become friendly, so I was teasing him as a friend. He was a long way from getting upset.

When I interviewed Ted Nugent for *TV Nation* he went ballistic a couple of times, called me a lying sack of shit and so forth. It's all in the finished story. But that's part of his schtick and I wasn't too worried about it. I had a weird moment on the porn shoot — which isn't in the final show — where I was interviewing a performer called TT Boy and he was getting uncomfortable and I didn't realise it. He went quiet and said, "I don't like your attitude." I was weirded out because it seemed to come out of nowhere.

Still, thinking about people ending it all due to the pressures of the porn business, don't you think Troy looked a likely candidate?

I couldn't really tell what was going on with Troy psychologically. Whether he's going to become one of those "psycho straight boys" is hard to say. I haven't heard anything bad about him since, though! On the contrary, I heard that Jon Dough, the performer with the motorcycle, had had some kind of run-in with the law on a domestic violence rap; and that Israel Gonzalez, the Elegant Angel cameraman who shoots the abduction scene, had had a shoot-out with cops and ended up turning the gun on himself. So it would appear that those two were more unstable...

For the readers, what's the name of the gay porn film in which you have a walk on part?[1]
It was taped under the title *Snowbound* but was released under the title *Take A Peak*.

There are a number of moments when people who appear relatively sane go 'lights out' and just change. This happens in the Survivalist programme, with the neo-Nazi who seemed to have a temporal lobe dysfunction in not recognising Mr Humphries in his favourite UK sitcom <u>Are You Being Served</u>? How unnerving was that whole conversation? It's pretty surreal too, what with you pushing him to say the catchline "I'm free!"?

That's maybe my all-time favourite TV moment of the stuff that I've done. I don't think he ever appeared even relatively sane, though, to be honest. Remember he looks out onto this mid-winter Idaho snowscape and says, "It reminds me of Cheltenham." My theory on what happened is that he <u>does</u> like Mr Humphries. I don't see how you could say you love the show and you hate Mr Humphries. It doesn't make any sense. So I think what's happening when he goes quiet and starts scratching his sleeve and appears not to recognise Mr Humphries is that he's thinking, "Oh, shit! I'm a neo-Nazi! I can't admit to liking Mr Humphries. What do I do now?" He's switching from Anglophile mode into hate-monger mode. It wasn't unnerving, though. It was exhilarating. I live for moments like that.

Did you have to appear to show some sympathy with the neo-Nazis to get into their camp?

No. They take it as a given that the media has no sympathy with neo-Nazis. They're not <u>that</u> out-to-lunch!

How difficult was it to remain objective throughout that sequence?

I don't think I did remain objective.

Going back to the first episode a moment, the Evangelist episode, how easy was it to set up a meeting with The Children of God (or The Family as they call themselves now)? They've been pretty defensive about themselves in the past.

My producer took care of that. They

Children of God on the streets of Europe in the Seventies.

took a little bit of convincing. But they've been on a mission to brush up their image, so they're not totally closed to the media.

The scene where you play George Michael's 'Faith' on your acoustic, and offer it to the group for their set is priceless. The head guy was completely baffled as to where you were coming from… but the young girls seemed to enjoy it! What was the atmosphere in that room like at that moment?

The atmosphere was slightly tense, more in the sense of embarrassment than in any dangerous way. It was like I'd just farted. I'd forgotten that the opening line is "I guess it would be nice if I could touch your body" — and I suddenly became aware that I was looking right at Steve, the head guy, when I said it. But I enjoy that kind of embarrassment in a TV context. It's very liberating.

Was 'Faith' the first and only choice of song you had?

I played 'Billy Jean' first, but it was hard to recognise because I didn't have all the chords down. So I switched to 'Faith', which is about the only song I can play all the way through.

Did Moses David[2] come up in any conversation?

They had photos of Moses David lying around and I asked about them. But we didn't go into detail. It was too off the point.

The Family relegated 'Flirty Fishing'[3] to being a thing of the past, which is evidently not the case when watching the way the girls act on the sidewalk that night. Any hint of other peculiar sexual practices in that household?

Not really. They marry very young. That's about it.

I can't imagine singing and preaching through the night on the streets of Deep Ellum you would have gotten away as lightly with hecklers as you appear to do in the film. How bad did it get?

Not too bad. Just drunk people hooting. No one threw anything.

Also in that episode, you appear on a televangelist's show live on air advocating that viewers in Britain were robbed of such shows. It's quite amazing that such subtle sarcasm was lost on so many people you spoke with. At any time did you or your crew nearly give the game away by sniggering?

That's one of the few moments in the Christianity show when I'm deliberately taking the

45

Main picture "I'm free!" Neo-Nazi before the conversation turns to Mr Humphries.
Inset Notice in the White Supremacist camp.

piss by saying something I know to be untrue. I think Joni Lamb, the televangelist wife, was suspicious right off the bat, which is why you can see I'm nervous talking to her. But for most of the Christianity stuff, I'm being genuine — all the stuff with Randy, for example, and Ann Lee, the "angels on your body" lady.

When we were interviewing Thor Templar, Lord Commander of the Earth Protectorate, for the UFO show, he was going on about how people were being apathetic about the alien threat; then he was talking about how it related to environmental damage, and out of nowhere he shouted, with the utmost indignation, "Seventy percent of the bees are dead!" I started laughing; I just couldn't help it. It was such a bizarre factoid and he said it so seriously. He got slightly annoyed but it was okay.

At any time in any of the shows, did you think 'I really don't need to be doing this?'
The frustrations come when a segment doesn't work out, because the characters are wrong or whatever, and these don't make it into the finished show. But for the show to work you have to take some chances, so it's inevitable they won't all pan out.

Were you ever asked to do anything that you were extremely uncomfortable doing? Were there any situations when you felt in danger?
The show's all about me being natural and responding in a natural way, so it doesn't work for me to be uncomfortable; and so we avoid those situations. Unless you count something like the scene where I'm being pressured to be born again by my evangelist friend Ann Lee. There I'm uncomfortable in a good way, because it's a natural human response to a difficult situation. Over all, I never felt I was in any serious danger.

Were there many groups or individuals that you attempted to contact but who refused to be filmed, or who said 'yes' but you didn't or couldn't show in the end?

We contacted Heaven's Gate before the mass suicide. They were very keen to work with us but said they had to focus on other projects. Then when they did kill themselves they sent us a package with their "exit" videotapes and a map indicating how we could find the bodies. We were their "preferred media contact." I wrote a story about it for British Esquire. We ended up meeting the last three survivors in Arizona but they weren't interesting.

Then we got inside a religious community with UFO beliefs called the Aquarian Concepts Community, also in Arizona. We spent a day and a half with them before getting thrown out. They didn't like my attitude, didn't want to be pegged as UFO believers. Remember this was right after Heaven's Gate so they were very skittish. It was a shame because they were a fascinating community.

For the Christianity story, we spent a day with Richard Keininger's community in Texas. He was part of the Stelle group in Illinois, a real old-style New Ager. He's written up in Donna Kossy's book Kooks. He thinks there's a good chance there'll be major disruptions come the year 2000 so he plans to take all his followers up in a fleet of blimps, to sit out the earthquakes and whatnot.

There were other people, too. For each two or three stories we use, there's another we don't use. Most of the people we contacted were very amenable, except for the televangelists. Of them, Marcus and Joni were about the only ones who would work with us. Televangelists have had too much bad press. Most of them aren't interested.

How much of an influence was the travel writing of your father, Paul Theroux, on <u>Weird Weekends</u>?
I'm a big fan of my father's writing, but as far as I know it didn't influence Weird Weekends.

Thank you.
I enjoy your magazine.

Sing-a-long-a-Louis.
Art © Dogger

notes

1. Louis plays the Mountie who comes knocking on the door of the retreat to warn of the impending bad weather conditions.

2. Real name: David Berg. The guy who started the Children of God.

3. One method the Children of God used to try and gain new members: females from the group would go out into the night and try and pick up men.

47

DENNIS COOPER DOES DRUGS

Stewart Home

T he Polo Bar on Bishopsgate is open twenty-four hours a day. The coffee is variable, so I usually order tea. I arranged to meet Dennis Cooper in this particular café because it is conveniently close to Liverpool Street station and three Jack The Ripper murder sites. Dennis is a Los Angeles-based novelist whose cult fiction explores his obsessional interest in young boys, sex murder, turds and bad pop music. Cooper's latest novel *Guide* (Serpent's Tail £8.99) contains a sexually explicit sequence featuring a thinly fictionalised version of Blur bassist Alex James. Cooper agreed to meet me if I'd plug the writing of his current boyfriend Michael Tolson, a twenty year-old junkie from Pittsburgh. Michael is looking for someone to publish his novel *Crap Hound*, more about that later.

As he stumbled into the café wearing an old jacket over a white T-shirt, a pair of cords and Timberlands, Dennis looked like he fronted an indie band, specifically The Fall. However, from the way he stared in fascination at a coffee stain on our table it quickly became apparent that Cooper didn't share Fall singer Mark E. Smith's penchant for booze. For a moment I'd thought Cooper was drunk but his boyfriend quickly corrected this erroneous impression. 'Dennis is tripping,' Michael explained. Several minutes after I'd asked if I should order coffee, Cooper mumbled 'Cool.' I took this to mean yes. Michael managed to pour coffee down his throat, Dennis spilled his down the front of his white T-shirt. At this point I decided to cancel an order for egg and chips. The café's staff appeared relieved as I coughed up the readies for the stuff we'd had and split.

It's weird to think that someone as spaced out as Dennis could get it together to write a novel. I asked him about this as we ambled down Artillery Row towards the site of Jack The Ripper's Dorset Street murder, now a multi-storey car park. My attempt to conduct an interview on the hoof was anything but satisfactory since whenever I put a question to Cooper I was lucky if I got a monosyllabic response. When we arrived at the murder site I described the carve-up of Marie Kelly in graphic detail. Dennis didn't seem interested, his attention was absorbed by a grease-stained Kentucky Fried Chicken box he'd plucked from the gutter. 'Awesome,' Dennis enthused as he turned this piece of litter over in his hands. Hoping for a better reaction elsewhere, I led Dennis and Michael up to Hanbury Street where Annie Chapman had been found lying on her back, hacked to pieces.

Dennis remained unmoved by the Jack The Ripper murders. He'd removed several bones from the discarded Kentucky Fried Chicken box and was subjecting them to a rigorous examination. This culminated in Cooper crunching the bones between his teeth. When I suggested we visit the site of another Ripper atrocity, Michael explained that Dennis was only interested in the murder of young boys and found hetero sex crime boring. Cooper was completely fried and there was no way he'd give me a coherent interview, so I put him in a taxi and told the driver to take him to Joshua Compston's flat on the Kingsmead Estate in Homerton. Compston was a Brit Art wannabe and two time loser, so I assumed he'd know the exact location of the notorious rent boy murder that took place very close to his pad a few years back. Young boys aren't my thing but I was left standing at the corner of Hanbury and Commercial Street with Michael as Cooper's taxi zoomed off.

'You can fuck me for the price of a fix,' Michael announced once Dennis had disappeared into the London traffic.

'I'm straight,' I explained.

'You're on another planet,' Michael shot back.

The kid might have been a permanent emotional wreck but he was sharp in the semi-educated manner of a teenage runaway who'd dropped out of school after reading a dozen William Burroughs books. Eventually we came to an agreement, I'd pay Michael £15 to have sex with a girl. Finding the girl wasn't difficult. She was nineteen and hooked on crack. Sabrina was wearing white shoes, dirty Levis, a matted sweater and her tangled black hair was a mess. Her beat was Commercial Street and her price was £20. We took a cab to a derelict property on Old Street. I'd acquired a set of keys to the building from a friend in need of a score. In the taxi Michael pulled a copy of his novel from a bag and handed it to me. This was useful since it gave me something to read as he shagged Sabrina. I didn't want to watch them get it on. Keeping Michael sweet was simply a way of staying tight with Dennis.

When Sabrina undressed I could see that her sallow skin matched Michael's. I focused my attention on the opening of Tolson's manuscript:

> I'd concealed myself in a doorway to do some investigative research by observing the punters going into Huysmans, a porno store in Hollywood. To help pass the time I fondled my parts. Eventually I clocked cult novelist Dennis Cooper scuttling inside. He was carrying a large box filled with old paedophile magazines. I instantly came in my pants. Twenty minutes passed before Cooper was out on the street again. I'd already come so the only way I could express my tremendous excitement was by shitting myself. A crack hooker standing nearby pulled a face and stomped off down the street complaining about scum lowering the tone of the neighbour-hood. Striding across the road towards the object of my lust, I savoured the deli-cious sensation of excrement oozing down my legs.

The novel turned out to be a parochial Beat effort. Imagine William Burroughs plagiarised by a porno hack who spends their spare time reading Harold Robbins and fantasising about making it with rock stars. I threw the manuscript down, placed seven five-pound notes on top of it and slipped out of the building while Michael was still grinding away on top of Sabrina. I've heard that somehow Dennis Cooper made it back to LA and is writing for the American Rock press. I've no idea what happened to his boyfriend.

five faces and a pair of missing eyebrows

Eugene Carfax

Leonardo da Vinci (c.1513), thought to be a self-portrait.

it has been said that the most defining faces of the twentieth century are those of Charlie Chaplin, Greta Garbo, Adolf Hitler, Mickey Mouse, and the Beatles. These five sets of faces are cited as being recognisable by a majority of the world's population far above any others. The statement appeared to hold good up until recently — and to them we might add Princess Diana, whom we will return to at the end. It now seems that our deep fascination with faces and the nature of identity is being recharted by a clutch of unusual and just as well-known faces which, in recent times, have come to embody a number of debates challenging our identity as a species and the gulf between established and unorthodox science.

In no particular order, these faces are: the alien 'Grey,' the image on the Turin Shroud, the facial structure on the Cydonia region of Mars, the Sphinx, and the Mona Lisa. I will touch on other facial images, but it is these 'big five' which preside over the summit of an Everest of thought and speculation, anthropomorphizing a host of fears and new disciplines of discovery in the twilight years of the second millennium. It is not my brief to argue whether the faces in question are 'real', or whether they show what the various sides say they purport to show. Rather, I prefer to discuss how there are a great number of curious parallels and interlacing links between the faces which looked at in total constitute an interesting alloy of fact and speculation.

The first and most obvious parallel common to all the faces is that their origins — their *true nature* — is subject to fierce dispute. The alien (and the word is not used to necessarily imply 'extra terrestrial') Grey is the star of uncountable articles, books, and reports ranging from those of sworn 'hardwarists,' presided over by a shady college of nuclear physicists and retired colonels, to the 'extra/intra-dimentionalists' who converse in a hybrid dialect of psychology and mythology: Without versus Within. Both polarities of thought have developed substantially in the last two decades: the hardwarists with much needed 'tangible' evidence in the form of the doubtful Roswell autopsy footage which emerged in mid-1994, and salivations over that infinitely speculative mad scientists' secret laboratory (in the mountains, to boot) at Area 51 in the Nevada desert. Not to be outdone, the dimensionalists too have forged towards a better understanding of the alien phenomena, their theories apparently supported in physics by multiverse models, and psychological insights into our collective archetypal roots and the prismatic, multiplicit nature of human identity.

So too, the Sphinx has been at the fulcrum of controversy. The strongest shots fired over the heads of modern orthodox Egyptology were in 1991 when Boston University geologist Robert Schoch published articles suggesting that the Sphinx was founded some 25 to 45 centuries earlier than mainstream Egyptologists assert, thus casting doubts on the presupposed techno-logical capabilities of the Nubian peoples, and the very cornerstones of modern archaeological thought.

Likewise — though not with quite the same ramifications — debate over the 'authenticity' of the Turin Shroud (i.e. whether the face it depicts is 'actually' that of one Jesus Christ) has evolved from the 'burst of radiation' speculation in the mid-1970s to the enticing model of the image being impressed onto the linen by some crude photographic method by Leonardo da Vinci (see: In Whose Image?), or failing uncomfortable facts regarding the shroud's age — carbon dated to the thirteenth century, too early for da Vinci — unnamed mediaeval 'forgers', as propounded by South African art lecturer Dr Nick Allen. If true, the Shroud shifts the dawn of photography to 500 years before its 'official' invention. Here, as with the Sphinx, orthodox history is being re-examined. Dissent is muted, at least from the Catholic Church who, while continuing to guard the relic with zealotry, have given up on their song that the image is a 'true likeness', certainly aware that they are no longer threatened with questions of 'authenticity'. If anything, they are enhanced. The Shroud is as miraculous and fascinating as ever.

The Cydonia face, a humanoid image over 2km in length, has also been the centre of an uneasy stand-off between orthodoxy and dissent since its discovery in 1976 by the Martian probe, Viking I. The pitch being drawn-up between astrophysicists and geologists, those closely associated with NASA and a growing group of dissenters, most visibly fronted by Richard Hoagland, centres on whether the face is of intelligent or accidental origin. Hoagland has produced persua-sive evidence drawn from the ancient science of sacred geometry and the emerging discipline of fractal geology to demonstrate how the Cydonian face is of intelligent origin. On the other side, NASA, who since the face's emergence have steadily been forced into a position of — if not a complete acceptance of Hoagland's ideas — a willingness to discuss the evidence. Their shift after nearly 20 years is perhaps conceded safe in the knowledge that a mission to revisit the site will have to be privately funded — and plans for this are in motion. The Cydonian face also calls into question the notion of perception, the horizon at which our neuro connections collapse visual input into familiar patterns. The first images we imprint are our parents' faces. Does this help us to understand the Cydonia phenomena's indisputable humanoid aspect? Are we seeing ourselves, exemplified by Sagan's infamous comment that the face is no more than a gigantic simulacra, akin to 'seeing Christ in a tortilla chip' or is the face of conscious, intelligent design? And if so, by who? At least two other faces have been noticed on the Cydonia plain; a grossly stretched face reminiscent of certain Polynesian masks, and one dubbed 'The Fox'. Doubtless more will be found, including the Tortoise, the Hare, and maybe even the Crestfallen Astrophysicist.

Questions of perception are also evident in the half millennia-old fascination with the Mona Lisa. The fascination with her smile (I could never really understand why) has sometimes obfus-cated a more intriguing puzzle: where are her eyebrows? (We'll return to that later.) Does, as has been written, the painting conceal the likeness of Leonardo da Vinci, a visual cipher for the Master's homosexuality? Computer-aided juxtapositions 'show' that the painting's features cor-respond exactly with that of an acknowledged da Vinci self-portrait, though we must be cautious as to what this actually means. The explosion of interest in the Turin Shroud, precipitated to world-wide effect by the VP-8 Image Analyser's evidence of 'three-dimensional information en-coded with the image' producing the striking sight of a man's body looking like the surface of the moon was less to do with 'encoded information' and more to do with the evolution of early 1970s computer graphics. Yet by the time this information was noted no one really cared; it just wasn't the point anymore. Reproduced everywhere, copied, lampooned, X-rayed, stolen, barri-caded and mobbed, subjected to a myriad of violations, the Mona Lisa remains a puzzle, a challenge to be 'decoded'. The identity of the sitter is disputed, so is the commissioner. Added to Leonardo's supposed 'infatuation' with the portrait, keeping it with him until his death, Napole-on's possessiveness of her (forget Josephine, it was Mona he shared his bedroom with every night), and there are all the tangents of a mystery that becomes more potent with each passing

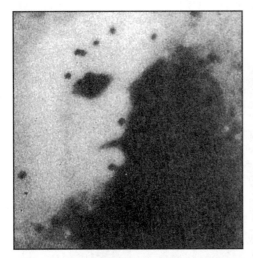

Left, top The facial structure on the Cydonia region of Mars. Left, below The Sphinx. Above The Mona Lisa.

decade. As Sir Kenneth Clarke observed, each generation is forced to re-evaluate its significance.

Thus, these five faces stand at the end of our age, representing the limits of our technology, our faith in various constructs of belief and empirical method, our grasp of history, our image of ourselves, and our readiness to accept other expressions of life. Yet, as I will go on to suggest, a clear understanding is perhaps only possible out of a wider picture, specifically how the five faces reflect each other.

Where the Cydonian face with its helmet-like garb appears militaristic, the face on the Turin shroud is at perfect peace. The royal headpiece of the Sphinx balances the sensible functionality of the Cydonian face's helmet. Just as the Mona Lisa and the Sphinx are amused (the Sphinx rather more *blissed*) — both revered as keepers of secrets — so the Grey looks like it wouldn't know a joke if one leapt up and bit its snub nose. The Mona Lisa and the shroud face are shy; the Grey and the Cydonian face confrontational. All exude a semblance of wisdom, regality, and each can be said to possess an aspect of beauty, even the Grey with its cold, insect hypno-symmetry.

It seems too obvious to mention, but each face holds itself up to so much scrutiny simply by virtue of their essential *stillness*. Efforts are made to gild, to give them a higher degree of realness. From Hoagland's flick-book rotation of the Cydonian face, to the shroud's 3D treatment, the Grey's realisation on television and movies — notably in the disputed Roswell footage — to the computer depictions of the Sphinx's weather erosion history, and the Mona Lisa's innumerable post-Beachamp fiddlings by artists and scientists. It is if the images themselves were not enough, as if the *prima* stillness of their design must be manipulated so that we can look around the back and see who's working the strings. No other faces have the power of such enormous fascination. Contrast their effect with the faces of movie stars. In the Studio Age, when images were rigorously controlled, great premium was placed on the publicity photograph, and in the era of silent films, declining after the introduction of sound, the power of the close-up exalted stars, to divine status, and the secrets of Hollywood makeup artists were guarded like Polaris launch codes. Nowadays there is precious little interest in what for centuries was a powerful technique of depicting royalty: the portrait. Royal portraits now are 'honest', and consequently viewed with contempt, subject to inquiry by experts on late night news programmes. As an experiment I recently denied myself all moving images for three weeks. Apart from a single lapse — two hours of frantic Italian television — I managed to expose myself only to still images. Upon my 're-entry' to my usual viewing habits, television and film images by contrast seemed incredibly amateurish. All the continuity mistakes, camera wobble, and mismatched cross-cutting of a drama were suddenly as vivid as if I were under the effect of an hallucinogen. For an hour the manifold *unrealness* of television was magnified. As television editing becomes more fragmented, the average cut now being around four seconds — far less in film trailers and the depiction of pop stars — it is as if there is a wariness, almost a *fear of stillness*. Even paintings on television cannot be displayed without a rostrum camera zooming, panning, splitting. Summon the emotions you felt when first seeing Clive Barker's cenobite creation, Pinhead. Experience Pinhead moving on film, then in still pictures. During movement and speech Pinhead's power to inspire fear is diminished; he teeters on comedy, too human, yet still images of him hold a mythic power that goes straight to the gut. Pinhead is a rare example of a face becoming popular on tattoos.

Of far more evident impact was the mass introduction of the Grey image through the brilliantly effective marketing of Whitley Strieber's **Communion** via a simple, almost childlike, painting. Paradoxically, we have a perfect example of the *density* conveyed

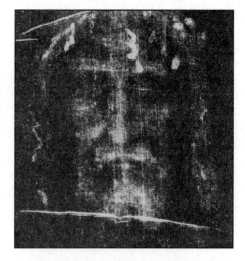

Top The face on the Turin Shroud.
Above The alien 'Grey'.

by a still image as opposed to movement when, in the movie of **Communion**, the Greys appear ridiculous and puppet-like.

Before I move away from stillness(!) I would like to briefly mention an example of a movie that contains images still resonant today. The movie is **Deliverance**, directed by John Boorman. Even those of us who have not seen the movie are at least aware of the celebrated 'Duelling Banjos' sequence played by the Appalachian mountain boy, Hoyt Pollard, opposite Ronnie Cox. Pollard's moon-like, Buddha's face was the result of a form of Fröhlich's syndrome, a condition produced by familial inbreeding and possessors are susceptible to altered states of consciousness. The pharaohs are now thought to have developed a form of Fröhlich's syndrome through generations of brother-sister intermarriages, the mental effects manifesting spectacularly in Amenhotep IV, later Akhenaten (c.1350-1334 BC), who converted the polytheistic religion of the time to a single solar-centred cult. Sculptures of Akhenaten clearly show his broad, almond-shaped eyes, a feature not at all dissimilar to the 'classic' Grey. At the end of the banjos sequence the defeated Cox ("I'm lost!") offers Pollard's character money but Pollard refuses, striking a haughty profile away from his bemused co-dueller and freezing in a profile reminiscent of Egyptian portraiture. Our final view of Pollard is on a bridge, swinging his banjo pendulum-like, as the city men float underneath, suggesting a preoccupation with time. For all intents, Pollard subsequently — and significantly, thus retaining his mystery — vanished, never to be seen again. This is a theme we shall return to. Several of Boorman's subsequent films dealt with Frazerian themes of the magic and danger inherent in the forest (**Excaliber, Zardoz, The Emerald Forest**) with markedly less successful results. Pollard's visual similarity to the ET that appeared at the end of **Close Encounters** — the most successful movie ever until **E.T. The Extra Terrestrial** — is beguiling. Now I am not suggesting that Pollard is an alien, but the blossoming web of connections bids us to consider which came first: the mirage or the oasis? The Disneyesque realisation of **E.T.** in several forms, one being a dwarf in a suit, was a secret closely guarded by the moviemakers, careful to retain the 'magical' realism of the creature until well after the movie had been injected into hundreds of millions of psyches. Looking back, it seems incredible the fuss that surrounded what was really a pretty weak movie. Image control was the key.

Since Jung's analysis of the UFO as a manifestation of an upwelling in the collective psyche, barely a week passes without a clutch of books purporting to reveal revelations of a divine impact revealed or channelled by aliens through 'chosen' messengers. The revelations vary considerably in detail, yet almost all deal directly with the origins of human culture, and the basic thesis is always the same: we're bigger than you, we've got the *real* answers.

The Turin shroud is now held up as a fake, commissioned by unknown powers to serve as visible proof of Christ's divinity. Yet the idea of a 'genuine' (i.e., a divine) miracle as opposed to a 'fake' (i.e., not a divine) miracle is a side issue in the wider context. What really matters is that the shroud emerged at a time of instability. The rate of expansion that had started at the beginning of the first millennium was at the point of breach in the fourteenth century. Famine was beginning to affect wider areas more frequently. Social instability catalysed by insurgences in the cities, revolts in the countryside, pestilence, fragmentation within the Church; all factors precipitating the emergence of the Shroud. Fourteenth century Italy was an overcrowded land exploited down to 'the last calorie, the last clod'. We can imagine the creators of the shroud diligently going about their work, galvanised with the doctrine that faith is best kindled by SEEING rather than HEARING because there is no intermediary; remove a filter and you are closer to the truth.

The substitution of The Word for The Image.

Contrary to the possible reasoning behind the Shroud's creation, 'proof' that the Cydonian face is the deliberate result of extra-terrestrial builders is seen as disturbing for the world's governing powers due to the 'snatched-rug effect', the sneaking worry that social cornerstones are threatened with collapse by a radical reinterpretation of history and the realisation that our governments are not really in control of the situation. The same applies to an eagerly anticipated hard 'proof' of the Grey's existence, major hopes being pinned on the existence of a 'Blue Book' supposedly delivered to the keeping of the US military by post-Roswell visitors. The rationale behind this is unclear. Would the same speculations of impending disaster be raised by a Cydonian foot, or an arm, no matter how accurately sculptured? It is curious how a feature containing such a high degree of symmetry and order can be thought to hold the means to such chaos.

The assumption that a mere face could hold the key to such damage reminds us how we automatically assume faces to be broadcasters of veracity: 'look me in the eyes and give it to me straight.' The race to develop viable video conferencing capabilities by computer hardware manufacturers is on, and real-time Internet dis-

This page Statue of Buddha (detail), 13th Century.
Next page Statue of Akhenaten, Louvre, Paris. When his tomb was rediscovered in the early 1880s, it was believed that the curious androgynous shape was that of a woman.

cussions will arguably remain a marginal hobby (wither thou, CB radio?) unless we are soon able to SEE who we are talking to since interaction without facial expression is considered incomplete. Who would consider hiring an employee on the basis of a job interview conducted over the telephone, or allow a witness in court to testify with just their voice? Presidents may not have to appear in court to give evidence, but they must still show their faces, albeit on video.

We must have hidden faces to counter those visible and, likewise, for those faces which for various reasons are violated, incomplete, and especially, those hidden, there is a stream of conjecture often as equally vigorous as that of their visible counterparts.

The Fulcanelli flurry in 1920s Paris, brilliantly stage-managed by a youthful alchemical-dabbler Eugene Canseliet and starving painter Jean-Julien Champagne with the publication of Les Mystère des Cathédrales, hinged on the fascination in esoteric circles on whether Fulcanelli — allegedly an alchemical adept 'on the verge' of achieving the Philosopher's Stone — existed in his own right or was a pseudonym for Canseliet, Champagne or one of a number of close friends interested in matters hermetic. The esoteric fraternity was tantalised with titbits about the Master. In the preface to Les Mystère des Cathédrales, Canseliet wrote:

> For a long time now the author of this book has not been among us. The man has disappeared and I cannot without sorrow recall the image of this industrious and wise Master to whom I owe all, while lamenting that he should so soon have departed.

The game was afoot: Find the Face. There were no shortage of players. In later years Canseliet boosted the Fulcanelli legend to even greater heights by claiming to have met his Master at a secret mountain retreat in Spain where he also encountered, fleetingly, a woman with Fulcanelli's face! In The Fulcanelli Phenomenon, Kenneth Rayner Johnson examines the tale, linking it with the Androgyne or Hermaphrodite, symbol of the dual nature of the Secret Fire and the end of the Great Work. This being is also represented as a twin-bodied lion with the single face, a comparable representation of the end of the hermetic process. In a side-thread to all this, Jacques Bergier has written of how in the summer of 1937 — five years before the start of the Manhattan Project — a stranger entered his laboratory and warned him of the dangers of working with nuclear energy, citing the experience of alchemists who had already probed the structure of the atomic nucleus. The stranger was said to have a 'metallic, dignified voice' which puts one in mind of the Men In Black who are also said to speak with a metallic timbre. In several famous cases, Men In Black are also said to have no eyebrows. Could there be an alchemical connection with the inter-dimensional Men In Black? The Mona Lisa, another Woman In Black, also has no eyebrows. Shall we chose to believe the official story that they were erased by a clumsy restorer or did she lose them in da Vinci's laboratory while bent over a volatile concoction? Or is there a deeper explanation?

Canseliet and Champagne (and Fulcanelli himself) could hardly have been unaware that if Fulcanelli stepped forward (or rather, showed his true *faces*) the interest in Fulcanelli's writings would have been distinctly limited. As it turned out, the initial first run of 300 copies of Les Mystère des Cathédrales, coupled with the story of the author's disappearance kindled international interest. The trouble is that, as soon as the word 'hoax' appears then all the good work is considered to be so much gossamer. It is the same with the Turin Shroud. The relic must 'either' be 'real' or 'fake', an unassailable chasm separating the two. Picasso once remarked that he as well as anyone could fake a Picasso. As to Fulcanelli, his pupil Canseliet must have the last word:

> Under the influence of that divine flame, *the former man is entirely consumed* [my italics]. Name, family, native land, all the

The <u>real</u> Stanley Kubrick.

illusions, all the errors, all the vanities fall to dust. And, like the phoenix of the poets, *a new personality is reborn* from the ashes.

The novelist Thomas Pynchon has been the subject of intense speculation (clumsily, 'Pynchonmania') centred, not around his work, but what he actually looks like. Ever since the late 1950s, the time of the last confirmed photograph of the writer, a growing body of fans discuss reported 'sightings' of Pynchon as if he were an aberrant natural phenomena, like ball lightning or the Bodmin panther. Grey hair, dyed hair, moustache, paunch, thin: without no face to see the Pynchonmaniacs shuffle identikit parts. Dozens of hard core fans have taken up the challenge of tracking him down. Similarly, the novelist J.D. Salinger has a famous dislike of being photographed, and when in 1985 a shot of a ranting Salinger was captured it was reproduced all over the world, sparking a revival of interest which could usually not resist wondering why Salinger was so jealous of his privacy — as if the wave of interest did not make it quite clear why he wanted out in the first place!

Director Stanley Kubrick retains a near-legendary mystique quite out of kilter to the quality of his work. Of course, 2001 A Space Odyssey is a near cinematic masterpiece and Dr. Strangelove, Paths Of Glory, and Lolita are fine movies. These aside (all made over 30 years ago), there's Barry Lyndon, A Clockwork Orange, The Shining, and Full Metal Jacket which I dare to submit are extraordinary patchy, even downright boring and dated works. Yet Kubrick preserves a mystique, bolstered by a famous reluctance to be photographed. The intensity of this reached its apogee in the late 1980s when an impostor who looked about as much like Kubrick as I do a Grey could pass himself off in restaurants as Kubrick and even give interviews to journalists.

The Man In The Iron Mask, the Kennedy Assassin(/s), Jack the Ripper — in each case enough research has been done to lay to rest with a reasonable certitude who these people really are and what they look like, but lacking proof on the magnitude of a time camera filming their nodal actions, popular opinion prefers these subjects to remain opaque, dismissing the best evidence as 'inconclusive' and defining the figure for the Nth time as 'shadowy' and 'elusive.' As yet another book about Jack the Ripper rolls off the press, the real psychopath who mutilated five women seems ever more superfluous to Jack the Shadow, the faceless broker of nightmares and blind-alley theories.

The host of bizarre customs and quasi-rituals surrounding criminals' faces and the need to remove them from public sight is evident in all cultures from the serial-killer leaving the police van draped in a blanket to the Doge's Palace in Venice where the portrait of traitorous doge, Faliero, is painted over with a black cloth. Or disguise: the odd assertion, unquestioned until his capture, that Carlos The Jackal was a 'master of disguise' when it was clear from photographs that he was about as proficient at self-concealment as Inspector Clouseau. The idea that he was somehow 'damned elusive' probably even served to fulminate a kind of collective blindness, assisting him to cross frontiers. Charles Manson and Ted Bundy changed their appearances many times, enhancing their legends far above more prolific murderers.

By way of the Mona Lisa, a woman who has no eyebrows, we come to our latent, seldom-confronted fascination with facial disfigurement. Two films, The Texas Chain Saw Massacre and Silence of The Lambs garnered wide notoriety, stemming in part from scenes in which the pivotal characters wear the facial skin of their victims. Gunner Hansen who played Leatherface in

Chain Saw is still in demand for magazine interviews and lectures to groups of avid horror fans — over 20 years after the movie was made! In the Jack the Ripper and Kennedy cases too there is a fascination with facial disfigurement that goes beyond basic morbid curiosity, elevated into the compulsion to 'decode' the facial injuries. Catharine Eddowes, one of Jack the Ripper's victims, has had the triangular cuts on her face interpreted to lend weight to a Royal/Masonic conspiracy in a development of Ripperology perhaps unthinkable before J.G. Ballard hinted at the codes contained within facial injury in Crash. In the Kennedy case, autopsy photos showing the complete face are challenged by conspiracy theorists who cite the seemingly contrary evidence demonstrated by the Zapruder film where Kennedy is clearly seen to lose part of his face. They may well be correct. The thought of the leader's face being blown apart is a disturbing contemplation, perhaps explaining why the full-face Kennedy autopsy photos/drawings were executed, not so much out of sinister desires to protect the Mob or LBJ, or Spook of the Week, or whoever, but to reassure the public that despite the shocking brutality of his murder *the leader's face remained intact.*

The regard in which the sacred power of certain faces are held is significantly evident in the Matilda Chapel, the Pope's private sanctuary in the Vatican. This building contains an image of Christ considered to be so holy that only the Pope is allowed to view it. This face has never been seen publicly, and resides, it is said, behind a veil. This is linked to the various African customs of veiling the face as a mark of sovereignty, the belief that to show one's face would mark a reduction in the divinely ordained power to rule. It is not unusual for movers in the upper social realms — usually nobility and high financiers, including members of Rome's elusive Black Nobility, or the secretive Reichmann brothers who backed the development of London's Canary Wharf — to be extremely assiduous in withholding their faces from public scrutiny. The Wizard of Oz's power rested almost exclusively in the projection of a false facial image.

Our five critical faces do not exist in a spatial vacuum. Each are sited within a personal landscape which contains certain mysterious and mythical aspects. The Grey's realm, whether outer space, parallel universes, the inner dimension of the mind, or some other dominion — perhaps a combination — leaves an uncertainty gap which to date has been bridged most accomplishedly in 'hard' terms by the legend of Area 51, 'Dreamland', a site now well-

Top **The Face of Christ**, a painting based on the image on the Turin Shroud, by Aggemian, 1953. This particular reproduction is taken from a 'stereo' postcard — the horizontal markings are courtesy of the Turin Shroud, the second image on the card.
Above Three-dimensional clay model, based on the face on the Shroud, made in 1963 by Leo Vala.

57

known for being 'the most secret location on Earth', perfect for speculation to rush in and fill the vacuum. Dreamland's closest urban neighbour is Las Vegas, the apotheosis of the urban dreamscape, raised in the space of a few short years from out of the Nevada desert by a mobster. The neon lights of the Las Vegas strip, once (if ever) considered glamorous are now revered as a high watermark of kitsch, and since the opening of the Luxor Hotel, a giant pyramid, complete with concrete sphinx, in 1992 has been injected with a needful — and immensely successful — sense of wonder by Douglas Trumbull's virtual reality experience, a simulated ride across a futuristic landscape. Those seeking fresh wondrous sights now have two options on entering Nevada: make to the top of the Luxor, or take the trip up to Area 51 and hope for a glimpse of lights in the sky as the military tests its ET booty. Trumbull was responsible for the blazing eye-candy in **Close Encounters Of The Third Kind**. Thus, the tip of the Luxor pyramid marks the terminus of a thread-weaving Grey lore, the duelling Pollard, and back, via the pharaohs, to the Sphinx who faces east to greet the rising sun.

The Sphinx inhabits a real physical landscape redrawn in mythical relief by astro-archaeologists and psycho-geographers. Not for any small reason does 'the Martian sphinx' ring act as an alias for the Cydonian face since the Avebury site, the centre of a major Neolithic development, is presently being studied by Hoagland and others for the unusual geographical correlations it exhibits with the Cydonia plain.

The Mona Lisa landscape is Leonardo's most quintessentially 'romantic' landscape, existing nowhere in Reality. Are those distant arches over the sitter's left shoulder supposed to be a sly joke, craftily balancing the missing arches, i.e. those damned eyebrows?

Would it be fanciful to suppose that before long we will have the opportunity to walk across the fractally-extrapolated 'moonscape' of the Turin Shroud, as others are already doing on simulations of Mars? What will we find in the canyons and plains of Christ's wounds? Pyramids, tetrahedronal forms? A simulacra of the Mona Lisa?

For myself, the mystery of all the five faces pivots not, I suggest, on their origins, but on their fundamental relationships with *light*. The sphinx faces the rising sun; almost all Grey visits are accompanied by blazing lights; the unwillingness of NASA to accept the Cydonian face on the assertion that the feature is 'a trick of light and shadow'; the Turin Shroud, now thought to be the product of light passing through a camera obscura over a period of several days, producing on the cloth a sort of hologram; and the Mona Lisa in whom da Vinci went further than anyone in perfecting his chiaroscuro technique, spending three years on the portrait to produce what J.G. Ballard has shudderingly called "the greatest movie of the twentieth century in the same way that **Gray's Anatomy** is the greatest novel". In his writings on light, da Vinci admits us to the core of his work:

> Shadows have their own boundaries at certain determinable points. He who is ignorant of these will produce work without relief; and the relief is the summit and the soul of painting.

There isn't time here to go into what is, from the point of view of this essay, the major event of 1997 — indeed the decade — the death of Princess Diana. The mythic dimensions to her life and death have already been covered by certain newspapers and publications, a new millennial watermark in the willingness of the mass media to discuss 'news' in mythic terms following Earl Spencer's invocation of mythic themes in his sister's funeral lament. Hopefully, the preceding thoughts will refract to show something of how I might approach this subject from a facial perspective. I was always moved by footage of Diana arriving at events in the evening, the way that her foot touching the ground as she stepped from her car sparked a nova of flash photography, an intensity of star-shell moments which rendered the light almost solidly white in her presence. The ravenous desire to capture her image proved fatal to her, demonstrating the inherent risks in being born with a face people want to possess.

Perhaps Diana should have followed the attitude more closely of one of our original icons, Greta Garbo, who, upon being asked by David Niven why she gave up the movies and shunned publicity said, reportedly after a long pause and almost to herself, "I had made enough faces." ◉

A return to Phil Tonge's
Cak-Watch!

A bumper crop of reader responses to Headpress 16's **Public Information Film** Cak-Watch! Plus... more **Animal Farm** anecdotes! Keep 'em coming!

On the subject of Public Information Films (PIFs), there is one that really stood out for me. It was shown sometime in the late-Seventies, when I was about 11 or 12-years-old.

It was actually premiered on *Nationwide* in front of a guest studio audience of kids, who were afterwards going to discuss their reactions. There was quite a bit of hype before its showing and prior to its screening it was announced that it was going to be especially harrowing, hence the reason my three friends and I sat with bated breath, nervously anticipating it and full of morbid fascination.

The film, I think, was called *Sportsday*, and it was British Rail's new weapon against hooliganism on and against its property. It was set on a school sports field, next to a railway line, and consisted of different sports events.

One event was for the teams to throw coloured stones at the windows of a passing train. Afterwards the camera moved down the interior of the train, collecting scores for each passenger hit by whichever team's coloured stones. There was plenty of blood and one team scored really well because they had hit the driver in the face.

Other events included a game of Chicken across the tracks of an on-coming train to disastrous effect, and another called The Tunnel Walk. In this, one team of children would run into the tunnel, seconds later a train would come hurtling out and then more children bearing stretchers would run in and stretcher out the bloodied bodies of the dead and injured.

Back on the playing field, the headmaster added up the scores after each event using a large scoreboard, showing how many dead and injured there were until finally there was hardly anyone — if anyone at all — left.

At the end of the film, when it returned back to the studio and the small audience of children, I remember Bob Langley having to ask if someone could help take out this poor white-faced kid who was about to vomit on live television.

My friends and I actually found the film to be quite disappointing, and the blood to be too unrealistically pink, but it fuelled our imaginations and we went out and made our

59

CHARLEY SAYS

MPI Video, 58mins, Cert. E (Exempt)

Containing 62 animated public information films as it does, I am amazed that this excellent video compilation has been sitting on the shop shelves for months without so much as a glimmer of interest from the press. As a result, sales must have been so poor that the promised second volume of live action shorts failed to materialise, and the MPI Video post office box has been cancelled. With two differing sleeves, I suggest you snap a copy up now as they won't be around for ever.

Interestingly, the five famous Charley Says adverts are among the weakest of the compilation, while the final — untransmitted — Protect and Survive short dealing with casualties following the Big Bang is frighteningly fascinating. Despite the laugh-while-you-learn attitude of many of these PIFs, quite a few stick with gut reaction and strong imagery. A mother leaving her baby unattended turns into the tortured creature of Edward Munch's The Scream at the sight of her pram overturning; smog becomes a deadly grim reaper and, without mincing words, Rabies Kills.

We are told on the sleeve to view the contents in retrospective context only. However, this is impossible as quite a few seem very topical: careers for mothers and young people, environmental issues, child molesters... On a trivial note, don't forget that "loosing your birds" is a direct result of not being able to swim, and if your yacht gets into deep water, God help you if only Joe and Petunia are watching. Thanks to Richard Taylor Cartoons and the voice of Kenny Everett (as Charley the incomprehensible cat), 1973 was the year paedophiles were forced to drop their much loved "Want to see some puppies?" chat-up line.

Voice-overs are supplied by celebrities like Prunella Scales, Wendy Craig, Arthur Lowe. Alan Bennett and Joss Ackland. But the best thing about this tape is that it comes without any unnecessary narration, interference or sarcasm. It's enough to make you positively nostalgic. David Greenall

own warped public information films on a Super 8mm film camera, consisting of plenty of blood, guts, vomit, mutilation and my cousin naked in a wardrobe.

Giles Clark, Surrey

Phil Tonge's hilarious PIF piece froze the lymph in my glands. I was absent from primary school when they showed *Apaches*, but even friends' subsequent descriptions terrified me, especially the kid-in-shit episode (drowning in quicksand, along with being kidnapped by men in balaclavas, were my most popular childhood fears at the time). However, I remember seeing *Building Sites Bite*. The teachers may just have well shown an animal-torture film, for all the good it did. The sight of a child straying onto an under-construction motorway, only to die under the wheels of an earth-moving vehicle, caused a severe bout of contemplation in me: why was there only a bloodied plimsoll left? Why didn't the driver *stop*? Years later, whilst working as a labourer, I had flashbacks of that other poor little bastard buried alive in an unshored trench.

Martin Jones, Devon

The PIF was the best Cak-Watch! to date. Regrettably I've only seen a few, but one or two seem to have been resurrected of late for TV. I do remember *Sparklers* from my youth, however, and one with a Cheggars voice-over about not accepting sweets/lifts/sodomy from strangers, starring a bloke in a car and a smug six-year-old girl. There was one we had to watch in middle school on two separate occasions. Some kid is flying a kite near train lines, and... well, go on, have a guess. It takes a good 20 minutes-or-so to set up plot and characters — presumably so its message will have more impact. The last shot is of the kid (Robbie, I remember his name) in hospital, his face obscured by his mum's head. She moves aside. He has a horrible great burn/scar across two-thirds of his face.

Quite a thrill for a nascent gorehound, but not much use as a cautionary tale for me: I lived in a middle-class suburb, miles away from a train station. Maybe the poor kids who lived in town got more out of it?

I could have done with seeing *Apaches*,

though. When I was about seven, the family went, as usual, to our relations' farm in rural County Down for a few weeks. I was pratting about on the farm on my own, and did actually fall into a big vat of pig shit. I probably would have drowned too, but my dad heard my screams. Can you imagine a more ignominious death? Last time I was there in 1995, I had a look at this dung repository, and felt a bit of a sap in retrospect; did I really come close to death in what was actually just about three feet of crap? Still, I was knee-high to a Time Bandit when it happened…

Anton Black, Rugby

I have a very vivid memory of losing my PIF virginity. I can't have been older than 12 or 13. These were exciting days: boys and girls had been separated for sex education classes (I sat at the back and giggled as we watched an 8mm film of microscopic fresh-water hydras bursting their testicles to release sperm. That was sex education, end of story). Space Invaders was all the rage, and I developed acne.

One morning just after registration, about 50-or-so pupils, myself included, were herded into the dark drama theatre and seated on the benches that steeply sloped up one wall. A projector was already in place half-way up the slope and a mobile screen in the centre of the ground-level stage. Only then were we informed that this was a screening of an important and 'educational' film that wasn't going to be fun or even pleasant. That's what they thought!

I don't remember the title, how it started, or the bulk of the action, but the message, climax and resulting mass hysteria is still crystal clear. The setting was a double-decker bus chock-full of boys and girls on their way to school, both sexes being somewhat boisterous with the narrator yelping for calm and warning all of impending tragedy. We sat in silence waiting for such a disaster to happen, and didn't have to wait long. One naughty young lass began to repeatedly press the bell on the upper deck, not knowing that four consecutive "ding-dongs" is a signal to the driver to make an emergency stop. The vehicle screeched to a halt throwing unruly children like rag dolls to the front of the bus. Although they were no fatalities, injuries were in abundance. Heads were bruised, arms broken, noses burst and legs gashed. The blood was bright red and gushed by the gallon.

Not only was this my first PIF, it was my first splatter movie. The boys lapped it up, the girls were mortified! No sooner had one girl fainted in horror, all girls in the audience began screaming their lungs out and dropping like flies. Teachers had to carry them out one by one. Due to this madness, I don't recall how the film ended, or if more screenings were held, but it was talked about in the school yard for weeks. The girls who passed-out were reduced to laughing stock. I presume teachers of future generations simply told their pupils not to fuck around on public transport rather than go through all that again.

All my other experiences of PIFs have been relatively recent and tame affairs, with all but one being restricted to the small screen. Both *Don't Let Him Die* (first aid) and the animated *Some Of Your Bits Ain't Nice* (personal hygiene) made by the Health Authority have their moments. A real gem however is the outrageously homophobic early-Sixties PIF *Red Light, Green Light*. Distributed by Denmark-based Jack Stevenson as part of his American vintage gay film show, *Red Light, Green Light* consists of six chilling encounters between child and child molester. A green light is superimposed on the faces of nice adults and a red light on the baddies. Interestingly, all encounters are same sex: women prey on girls and men on boys.

You don't seem to come across PIFs on television anymore, but this was the best way to see them as they pounced out from nowhere at 3am. The last one I saw was about six years ago while watching late night trash TV. It began with an old lady looking up at a light-fitting with a dead bulb, out come the wobbly step ladders, and without a friendly neighbour to hold the ladder steady, she makes her ascent — only to fall through the doors of a wood and glass display cabinet before hitting the floor (in slow motion no less). Shocked? Indeed I was! Laugh? I almost wet myself.

David Greenall, Manchester

Phil Tonge's CAKWATCH rekindled memories of several PIFs not included in his piece. How about *Don't Put Stuff In High Places*, where several scenes of old folk struggling to reach things climaxes with an old man standing on a rickety dining table to reach his box of memories from the old wardrobe. Cue Granddaughter waving through the bay window. "Granddad!" she cheers. The old geezer turns and slips, freeze-frame on his tumbling body. Our imaginations do the rest — a clever technique. This PIF especially fascinated my friends and I. We pissed away hours of school perfecting Granddad's final yelp, a kind of strangulated "WAEE!"

Another PIF with a classic freeze-frame ending was *Gas Goes Bang* where a couple return home (after carefree romantic dinner?). The woman is about to switch on the light, but the man's nose is twitching to the funk of leaking gas. "NO!" he barks, nanoseconds away from the spark-lit suburban inferno. Again, hours of fun mimicking that final pose and "NO!"

The Spirit of Dark Water, as Phil rightly point out, is a horror classic. Grislier though was *It's Not Chocolate!*, starring Dr David Bellamy. Kids get in some filthy horrible places, don't they? But here's Dr B explaining why you don't go near dog poo, or touch your eyes with soiled fingers. Shots of toddlers falling in the stuff, picking it up (eating too?). Dr B's absorbing commentary exposes the various kinds of bacteria present in dog cak. At the very end, if memory serves, we're left with a mid close-up of a child's turd-smeared face and hands. I saw this one at school as part of my 'Design For Living' course. Harrowing.

Want a PIF Night on BBC2? Write to Mark Thompson, Controller BBC2, Room 6066, TV Centre, Wood Lane, London, W12 7RJ.

Thomas Blacktree, London

"When the old man's away…"
Art © Tom Brinkmann

Letters are still rolling in on the nature and supposed origins of Seventies bestial atrocity, _Animal Farm_ (including one scurrilous rumour that its director is now a prominent British top-shelf mag publisher — unlikely). Here are the latest…

TOM BRINKMANN, USA I've had a run-in with a film loop taken from *that* movie. I found the said film loop in the trash a few years back. Being "thrown for a loop" by it because of its bizarre nature, I took the opportunity to render some high contrast drawings from some of its more poignant moments and thought I'd share these with you [this page and below], along with the little bit of info I have concerning it. The text at the beginning of the loop is as follows: "Color Climax presents Film no. 1267 'ANIMAL GROTESQUE' © 1972." On the 'leader' film before the thing starts properly is scratched 'Head' Pig.

I suppose most would say this should have been left in the garbage where it belongs, but I think of it more in terms of cultural anthropology — albeit underground culture.

ANTHONY FERGUSON, AUSTRALIA I came across a copy of *Headpress* in a local alternative music/bookstore here in Canberra. Very much enjoyed the articles on sex and death. Just a few comments on Phil Tonge's review of *Animal Farm*. You'll be pleased to know this film has surfaced down under. I first encountered stills from the film back in 1979 when searching through my dad's porn collection one afternoon. They were contained in a mag called *Animal Bizarre* if I remember correctly. Wiggy was there, as were three girls and a collie, and a couple of birds with either a horse or a pony.

Back in 1991 when living in Western Australia, I gave a blank tape to a workmate, who proceeded to pirate tape a couple of porn films for me. As there was about 40 minutes spare tape he filled it with the very film discussed in your publication, or at least excerpts from it. Unfortunately, I no longer have the video as I lent it to someone last year, who lent it to someone else... and well you know the rest. I never saw it again.

Anyway, it was all there. As I remember it starts off with the general farm shot, a few animals, no titles or credits. Wiggy shows up, as does the bird with the awful perm. My memory may be blocking most of it out, but I'm sure I recall Wiggy doing both a heifer and a chicken. There was the collie scene, one with a horse, and I swear, a scene with two girls dressed as nuns getting friendly with some pigs. I distinctly remember this as the pigs had corkscrew dicks. This scene may have been spliced on, however.

As for the film's origin, it always struck me as Dutch or German. I think only they could have produced something as offensive as *Animal Farm*. I'd be surprised if it was English. But then, you did elect that Tory Government full of sexual deviants for two decades.

"The 'slattern' in a pensive mood."
Art © Tom Brinkmann

GILES CLARK, UK Issue No 33 of *Oz* magazine, dated February/March 1971, has an interview conducted by Ole Ege — co-director of the animal sex film *A Summer Day* — with its actress, Bodil. She is described as "a strapping 25-year-old Danish girl, famed throughout the length and breadth of pornography as the girl who makes it with animals".

I don't know how reliable this interview is, but the best quote is "she claims to be happy, because her pay from the photographs and films that she does means that she can afford her 40 to 60 cigarettes a day".

A few years back, I used to share a large house with a group of young student nurses and one of the girls used to enquire whether I would be able to get hold of a copy of *Animal Farm* for her.

I've never seen it myself, but in 1985 a couple of my friends were able to get hold of a video called *Horse Lovers And Dog Lovers*, which consisted of two not-bad-looking girls with a collie dog and one fattish girl with a horse. One of my friends found this all too much and had to run out of the room.

Then while one of my same friends was living in Sweden in the late-Eighties, he was able to borrow a tape from the local video shop consisting of two male and female couples and one big black dog. One girl had to go down on the dog, but was timid about getting her mouth around its dick because it kept squirting out piss. In the end she just closed her eyes and went for it. My friend says this was fantastic!

I've seen the Cicciolina film mentioned in the last issue, which we found inserted part-way through a tape of normal porn. From what I remember, the girl sucking the horse's dick was gagging quite a bit from the experience (it wasn't Cicciolina — she was having sex with some guy next to the horse, and so were a second couple). I watched this film with my friends, and we all came to the conclusion that they used a badly made

"The function of the orgasm?!"

Art © Tom Brinkmann

artificial dick for the moment when the horse actually cums over the girl. The funniest part for me was at the end, when they put the horse back into his stable, pat him on his nose, and then all five climb happily into a small Italian hatchback car and drive off while waving goodbye to the horse.

DR MARK GRIFFITHS. PSYCHOLOGY DIVISION, NOTTINGHAM TRENT UNIVERSITY Back in 1986, I was a psychology undergraduate at the University of Bradford and like many of my friends took a very healthy interest in all things sexual (in fact my first dissertation was on the psychology of female orgasm). Your recent articles on *Animal Farm* brought back my own memories which I thought I would share with *Headpress* readers. However, I must stress that my recollections are from over 12 years ago and are a little vague to say the least.

I used to live in a house with eight other guys, one of whom worked in his spare time at a local video shop. Every Sunday, he used to bring home a selection of 'under the counter' videos featuring hard-core pornography with titles such as *Anal Schoolgirl* which we as a group used to sit around and watch. One Sunday in March 1986, he brought a video which I remember as being called *Farmyard Stories*. It certainly wasn't called *Animal Farm*. I also remember that each 5 to 10 minute scene was given its own title. The first one was simply called "Chicken Fucker" and is identical to the accounts that other *Headpress* readers have given involving a man having intercourse with a chicken. I must admit that when the camera did a close-up of the chicken's rear-end after this particularly depraved act, I was left feeling repulsed and wondered who the hell got kicks out of this kind of material! I had forgotten all about this until recently when I watched John Water's *Pink Flamingos* featuring its own chicken sex scene!

The second vignette I remember quite clearly was entitled "Snake Fucker" but con-

"Contemplative."
Art © Tom Brinkmann

cerned eels — not snakes. I remember a lesbian scene in which one of the women tried to insert live eels into the vagina of the other (and had great difficulty doing it). My memory is a shade hazy but I seem to remember that they killed the eels in the end and inserted them vaginally. What I do remember quite vividly was the eels being cooked and served up to a guy who on eating them suddenly became sexually rampant (the idea being that the eels took on an aphrodisiac quality as a result of being smothered in vaginal secretions). There was then a scene of 'normal' hardcore sex interspersed between what had essentially been a bestiality film.

A third story was (I think) entitled "Wild About Horses" and involved two women and a horse. I cannot remember that much except that one of the women ended up fellating the horse while the other one was stroking the horse trying to keep it calm. I seem to remember that the same outdoor field scene involved one of the women being mounted by a dog and where the dog copulated with the woman for what seemed like a couple of minutes. I'm sure this was not a separate segment. I also remember that the dog was given fellatio by the other woman. Very weird and not something I particularly want to remember!

I cannot remember any other vignettes although there were some others as the 'film' (actually just a series of unrelated bestiality scenes) seemed to go on for about an hour. ◉

66

"Bliss… Looking not unlike Keith Richards c. late '60s/early '70s."
Art © Tom Brinkmann

HANGING WITH FRANK

David Graham Scott

'I was put on this earth to do this work.'
Albert Pierrepoint,
British State Executioner 1931–56

Mr Frank McKue is a very likeable fellow. Sit with him in his local and he'll chat away quite the thing. Frank will, however, always turn the conversation to a subject most dear to his pig-valved heart: hanging.

I first met Frank a couple of years ago when I was doing research for a documentary about the old gallows in Barlinnie Prison, Glasgow. This forbidding jail dominates the skyline of its east end locale. Notorious American killer Carl Panzram even spent some time there back in 1919. There were 10 men, however, who were destined to never leave this place — their unmarked graves a testament to that fact. I needed as much information about these characters as possible. But the gentlemen who had disposed of them had passed on, and there were next to no records of the executions within the prison or contemporary newspapers. (It was both strange and disconcerting to view the scant columns devoted to these judicial killings.) So it was a great boon to my project to discover a man who had personal memories of the execution procedure and the last days of the condemned: ex-death watch officer Frank McKue.

Frank was a fountain of knowledge when it came to capital punishment. On the Scottish hangings this century he'll rattle off crime details, dates of execution, the prisoners decorum in the condemned cell and on the scaffold, but most importantly the executioners involved. You see, Frank is very interested in executioners. Interested to the extent that he actually wants to be one. He's counted great British hangmen such as Albert Pierrepoint,

Window in the death chamber, Barlinnie Prison.

Photo © David Graham Scott

Syd Dernley and Jock Stewart among his friends. He can take you into his 'special room', devoted to crime and punishment, and show you his filing cabinet — an A–Z of executioners and methods of execution. Death by hanging is his favoured form of execution. He knows exactly how it's done and he wouldn't lose sleep fastening a rope around your neck and dropping you to eternity. He'd even send his best friend through those trapdoors if he had to. No, you can't let personal involvement get in the way of a good execution.

There's a tale recounted by Albert Pierrepoint which aptly proves this point. It's the Tish and Tosh story you'll find in Albert's memoirs and it goes something like this: a condemned prisoner by the name of James Corbitt had been excitedly boasting to the death watch officers that he was a personal friend of Albert Pierrepoint. This man had actually been a regular at Albert's pub 'Help the Poor Struggler' in Hollinwood, near Manchester. Part of his drinking patter involved greeting the landlord with the phrase 'Hello Tosh' (a contemporary catchphrase). The same lively, easy-going chap strangled his girlfriend one night, scrawling the word 'WHORE' across her forehead in pencil. Now in the condemned cell of Strangeways Gaol, James Corbitt was growing restless. He feared Albert wouldn't recognise his old friend. Well, on the big day, executioner Pierrepoint and his assistant entered the condemned cell to prepare the prisoner for the scaffold. Corbitt wheeled round and a 'Hello Tosh' was uttered. Though quite startled Albert immediately responded with the expected 'Hello Tish'. The condemned man breathed a cheerful sigh of relief and went lightly to the scaffold. Anxious to please his old pal, the pinioned man even tried to ease his head into the noose to help matters along. Albert rearranged the hood on him, jumped over to the lever and without a moment's hesitation sent him on his way.

'I'd drop any one of them if I had to,' says Frank as he gestures towards his drinking cronies. As if to reassure his pals he points an ominous finger towards me. 'Yes Frank, I guess you'd drop me too if you had to.' 'If Albert could have done it, that's good enough justification for me., Apparently, however, Albert was a joy to be with, a really nice guy. Frank visited him in his last years when he was confined to a nursing home. Rumours abounded over Albert's obsession with knots and tying up shoelaces. With faithful devotion to his idol, Frank denies all such stories. However, he'll quickly side-step the fact that Albert Pierrepoint had extreme doubts on the effectiveness of Capital punishment: 'I do not now believe that any one of the hundreds of executions I carried out has in any way acted as a deterrent against future murder. Capital punishment, in my view, achieved nothing except revenge.' (Pierrepoint A., *Executioner Pierrepoint*, p.10, Coronet Books, 1977). It took him over 300 executions[1] to realise that point.

'I'm still on the list of persons approved to train as an executioner,' Frank proudly boasts. His name has graced this list for over 20 years. It's obviously frustrating for the poor guy, waiting all that time and not able to fulfil his dream of hanging someone. When

Frank McKue practicing hangman skills.
Photo © David Graham Scott

Hanging with Frank

dir/pr: David G. Scott, 1996

In the autumn of 1995 former death officer Frank McKue returned to the execution chamber of Barlinnie Prison to view the facility before its imminent destruction.

So opens this short film (approx. 10 minutes' duration), which follows Frank McKue on the sentimental journey noted in the above titles. Big Frank makes no attempt to veil his sorrow at the thought of the Barlinnie death chamber standing derelict, covered in pigeon shit, and about to be brought down for good. He has a blinkered drive and determination to *hang 'em high*. (See main text for details.) When the interviewer queries the validity of capital punishment, raising the issue that some individuals have been wrongly executed in the past, Frank answers with mindless aplomb: "If you're 100 per cent sure — hang them."

The execution chamber itself is split into three levels. At the top is the 'beam room', where the ropes would be fastened come the big day. At ground level the actual hangings took place (the bodies would be left suspended for one hour), and directly beneath this is the 'slab room', where there would be a slab on which to place the deceased, and a coffin to take him away in.

At the sight of the demolition men taking the chamber apart, Frank admits to being "quite emotional".

Barlinnie Prison had the capacity to execute three men at a time, but all of the 10 hangings that took place there were individual executions. Outdoors, along one wall of the prison, lie the part-demolished graves of these 10 men. Frank wanders by them, rattling off from memory the names of the deceased. He hesitates at one grave, suddenly unsure of the name of the man who lies therein. But he remembers it later, part-way through another conversation.

A fine documentary. **David Kerekes**

I recently showed him a newspaper sideline concerning the overcrowded death rows of some tinpot African state he rubbed his hands with glee. He imagined himself taking on the urgently required executioner's job and clearing the backlog of several hundred prisoners.

Just how this wheezing old geezer with a dodgy ticker was supposed to dispatch even one of these strapping African lads was well beyond me. Nevertheless, he pointed out that Tom Pierrepoint was a hangman right into his seventies. True, but the hard Yorkshireman who trained his nephew Albert in the hangman's skills was said to be 'all broken up and one gets the impression his heads and hands are about to fall off'.[2]

Clearly it's important for Frank to have his dream. He'll recount in detail the meticulous procedure involved in preparing the scaffold and prisoner for 'the perfect drop' just as if he were a practising hangman. In my short film, *Hanging with Frank*, I gave Frank the opportunity to bring the decayed structure of the Barlinnie gallows briefly back to life. He takes us from the condemned cell, across the landing to execution chamber and recalls the

Left The hanging room.
Right Grave site for one of Barlinnie's
condemned (partly excavated).

Photos © Tom O'Brien / David Graham Scott

exact process as the prisoner is guided to the trapdoors. The T-mark is chalked up for the prisoner's feet to be set against. That makes him dead centre on the trap. The hood is placed over the head and a rope of ¾" Italian hemp is tightened around his neck. The rope's length has been calculated according to a table of drops to ensure the prisoner dies without strangling or decapitation. The knot of the rope is placed underneath the left jaw to throw the head back — the rope always making a quarter turn as it falls taut — and the prisoner's neck is cleanly broken between the second and third vertebrae. 'And that was him instantaneously dead.'

But that isn't the end of the story as far as the hangman was concerned. Frank recalls the general procedure after an execution: The body would be left hanging for one hour after being certified dead. This was a precaution as it was said the heartbeat would some-times continue for up to twenty minutes afterwards. The executioner and his assistant would then leave the death cell and have their breakfast. On returning, the body would be lowered down into the pit below[3] and laid out on the mortuary slab. He was then stripped and washed and sealed in a special coffin. The corpse was covered in quicklime and water was poured through a special flap over the face to activate the process of disintegration. The body belonged to the state so it was buried within the prison grounds. Ashes from the boiler house were used to fill the graves which were frequently topped up due to the decay of body and coffin. Frank helped organise these grave filling expeditions. He noted that there were instances where the corpse was actually mummified by the quicklime. It was quite a simple procedure to grind it down with his boot.

The Scottish Prison Service Authorities sounded the death knell for the old execution suite when they announced the structural improvements necessary for Barlinnie Prison. The former gallows would now form upgraded cells for the burgeoning prison population. Frank was pretty depressed on the day we returned to view the demolition. The gallows beam had been removed, the floor of the death cell ripped up and the graves of the 10 men executed there were lying open. We could see large drainage pipes leading from the newly-built toilets running through the graves. Not only would they never leave the prison, they now had to face the indignity of being shit on every day. Frank looked about in dismay: 'It can never, ever be rebuilt again. It really upsets me. It's just like taking the Scott Monument[4] out of Princes Street, terrible... just terrible.' There was some consolation however. The forthcoming Scottish parliament has promised to discuss the subject of capital punishment. Frank muses upon this. Yes, perhaps there was one last chance for Mr Frank McKue to become Executioner Number One. He laughs, orders another pint and a nip, and patiently waits to serve the people of Scotland.

Frank surveys the demolition of his beloved gallows, June 1996.
Photo © David Graham Scott

1. Most of these were war criminals in post Nazi Europe. He once hanged 27 in the space of 24 hours. Pierrepoint also taught the Austrians the drop method of execution, replacing their archaic method of clinging on to the prisoner's legs to hasten death.

2. This quote is attributed to Master Sgt. John C. Woods of the US Army. Woods became notorious for the bungled executions of the leading Nazi war criminals at Nuremberg 1946. Noses and lips were torn from faces as they dropped through the trap and several took up to 20 minutes to die from strangulation. These were Woods' last hangings — the stress making 'an old man of him'.

3. A sandpit below the trapdoors was designed to catch any body fluids.

4. An Edinburgh landmark.

Beautiful lettuce pages

Your fascinating Skywald piece [see **Headpress** 16] brought on retro thoughts: my childhood years were taken up by **2000AD**, **Battle/Action** and the unbelievably shite **Eagle**, but do you remember **Misty**? Aimed at pre-pubescent would-be gothettes, and those of us frightened by **Tales of the Unexpected**.

Martin Jones
Devon

Do you remember El Lunatico from 'The Saga of the Victims' (**Scream** 9, I think...)? A Nazi midget riding the ocean in a robotic giant squid?...

Mark Farrelly
London

Hooray! Yes — Skywald!! I got **Headpress** 16 today and I must congratulate you on having such 'great taste'. I love horror comics: 1950s pre-code titles, 1960s–70s black & white comic mags...But my absolute favourites are the Skywald titles. Nothing else approaches them for weirdness. There's almost a spiritual-queasiness about them, particularly from **Nightmare** 8/**Psycho** 7

onwards, when 'Archaic' Al Hewetson really began to express himself.

My first introduction to Skywald was on the day of my oldest sister's wedding. A family friend took me out of the way of the hubble and bubble of important matters to the newsagent, where I saw a copy of **Nightmare** 5. One story in particular, 'Slime World' by Chuck McNaughton and Ralph Reese, played havoc with my imagination for the next few weeks! I wish I still had that issue — it's one of the few missing from my Skywald collection. (At least I've got 'Slime World' though — it's reprinted in the 1974 **Psycho** annual.)

A couple of years passed, and I was 11 or 12-years-old before I came upon **Nightmare** 16. After that, I got as many issues as I could afford (not so many in those days), despite tacit parental disapproval. About 10–12 years ago I put an ad in a comics trade magazine and managed to get nearly all the lot. As a comics fan, I was shocked by the omission of Skywald titles from Duncan McAlpine/Titan's **Comic Book Price Guide** — a situation I attempted to rectify by contributing to the project, editions 1994/95 and 1996/97, providing the low-down on Skywald and other obscure matters. Though I was rightfully credited as a contributor, the Skywald material was totally ignored, and the current, exhaustive (sic) edition of the book still omits any mention of Skywald's entire 1970–75 magazine line, though Warren's **Creepy**, **Eerie**, **Vampirella** and **Famous Monsters** (why??!) are now featured. Are the Horror-Mood mags just too unsavoury and weird for most comic fans' tastes...?

Stephen Sennitt
Yorkshire

Panels from Skywald's incredible <u>Slime World</u> strip.

Art © Ralph Reese

In response to C. J. Turner's excellent and amusing obsession with Gerry Anderson Babes [see **Headpress** 15 & 16], I recall that Lt Green used to entertain the Angels with his Caribbean calypso guitar. I read this in his biography in a **Captain Scarlet** annual and for some reason (initial penis envy of black men nurtured from childhood?), it stuck. I also think that in the biography of Captain Blue, there were at least two Angels who he was 'very popular with' (can't recall which ones — symbolic of getting boys into the idea of a threesome?), and that Captain Scarlet, surprise surprise, was popular with 'all the Angels'. (Fucking typical! Indestructible **and** on for group sex sessions!!) As for **UFO**, I always wanted to see Gabrielle Drake (Lt Ellis), on duty with Skydiver so I could clock her in a string vest. Check out dusky babe Dolores Mantez as Lt Nina Barry in 'Sub-Smash', and you'll see the possibilities. When she crawls out of the crash dive tube, sweating, dirty, clothes torn, breasts heaving... However, my 'all time top of the pile' **UFO** babe is the bit part of 'SHADO operative', played by Ayesha. She's the one giving the sexy little wave in the opening credits. Some of you may remember the Asian stunner from her Saturday morning show (pre-**Tiswas**), **Lift Off with Ayesha**.

Oh yeah, a friend of mine voluntarily admitted in conversation that he thinks his peccadillo for Oriental babes stemmed from Tin Tin in **Thunderbirds**. What a nasty can of worms we seem to have opened up...

H.E. Sawyer
Essex

I think **UFO** sparked off a lot of fetishes in young kids during the Seventies, I know it affected me (I'm 27) — I get the hots for silver catsuited ladies now! Here's a picture of my wife [above].

Chris M.
Birmingham

Since my early teens I have been obsessed with an unusual portion of the female anatomy — the humble navel. Growing up I was drawn to (and searched out) any books, magazines, videos that featured girls displaying their navels, and found their images far more arousing than any porn. I've been quite open about my fetish. Over the years, various girlfriends have been subjected to my desires and have been surprisingly accommodating. Indeed I even seem to have turned some of them onto the same thing! But things have taken a sinister turn. Recently, cable channel 11 (UK Living — a crap station I would never normally watch) screened a two-part pilot, heralding a new police thriller series. It was called **Murder Call** and was basically an Australian rip-off of **Cracker**, with a relatively attractive female police officer in the Robbie Coltrane role. I caught it by accident as I surfed the channels.

No point going into explicit plot details, the programme isn't worth it, but what caught my interests was a scene featuring an attractive woman lying on her back, in bed (quite dead and fully clothed), the white handle of a knife protruding from her stomach. In the background, a police officer was saying something like, "... a steak knife straight through her navel..."

I found it incredibly arousing, possibly the most erotic scene I have ever witnessed. The next day, in episode two, we were allowed to see the victim in the morgue (fully dressed) as police officers discussed the case. The pathologist moved in to examine the body and I was virtually paralysed before the screen, praying for an in-depth shot that would reveal the navel wound in graphic detail. Of course it didn't happen. And there you have it. My fetish has ascended (descended?) to a new level. I find myself desperately searching for films or literature that feature scenes of violence committed to (pretty) girls' belly buttons.

Anonymous

*What's the **matter** with you people? — Ed.*

I have been following **Headpress** since about No 5. The change into the new format has been great and anything that you do to add more info and create a fatter publication, well hooray, I'm all for it. Just one thing: I generally can't wait for my mates down at Freaky World to inform me that the new **Headpress** is available as it is; if I had to wait six months I think I would go mad.

Andrew Lount
<A.Lount@derby.ac.uk>
See page 75 — Ed.

write Headpress, 40 Rossall Avenue, Radcliffe, Manchester, M26 1JD, Great Britain email david.headpress@zen.co.uk

S.H.K., R.I.P.

Art this page: SHK

Sverre Helmer Kristensen, comic book artist and editor/publisher of *Sewer Cunt*, died November 5th 1997, after two-and-a-half years of struggle with blood cancer. After the first round of heavy treatment, in the summer of 1996, he was apparently well. He travelled to London, and created a design for a T-shirt that said "God Tried to Kill Me, But He Couldn't Do It!" But he suffered a serious setback, had to undergo another round of treatment, and by 1997, he was told he couldn't be cured.

He had to go to the hospital in Aarhus every four days to get a painful injection directly into the spine, and it was on one of these visits that he collapsed and died.

In addition to the vast amount of comics he drew, Sverre also made the cut-up style documentary videos *Something New To Die For* (about the Church of the SubGenius) and *No Sense Makes Sense* (about Charles Manson). These were shown at video festivals around the world (including one in Iran!!!) and got great reviews.

Sverre grew up in Copenhagen, Denmark, and in his youth he lived for some years in Sunnmøre in Norway. Then he moved back to Denmark and went to art school in Kolding for four years. The other students concentrated upon industrial design and other potentially money-making directions, while Sverre did as much drawing and weird videos as he could.

His comix career mostly consisted of un-compromising self-published work, but he also had comix published in the Canadian anthologies, *Kekrapules* and *Compendium Comix*, along with artists like Julie Douchet, Joe Matt and Mike Diana. SHK-only comic books (by various publishers) include the titles *Det*

Magiske Cirkus and *Donald Fuck*. In the late-Eighties he did quite a lot of colour covers, comix and posters for the Norwegian version of *Mad*.

In the Nineties he worked for a company which manufactured children's clothing. A lot of cute cows and dinosaurs drawn by SHK can be found on these clothes. Quite a departure for an artist who was otherwise obsessed with drawing comix about death, murder, torture and rape. He didn't like this job very much, but it provided a steady income, and he used his employer's computers to do layout on *Sewer Cunt*.

One of Sverre's 'idols', Church of Satan founder Anton LaVey, died exactly a week before him. But LaVey's family kept the death a secret until November 5th, the day Sverre died. A twisted synchronicity he would have loved.

His partly autobiographical 60-page comic book *Bad Pills* is published by the US publisher Mike Hunt. It contains a story about 'King Kancer'. However, 'Almost Dead', an autobiographical story about the time of his illness, was pulled by Sverre just before he died. (It might see publication at a later date.)

A 40-minute best-of Anus Presley CD that SHK named *Music to Listen to When You're Dead* will be issued by Jazzassin in Norway.

A close friend and collaborator on many projects, he will be missed a lot.

JR Bruun

Editor's note I asked JR Bruun what some of these collaborations between himself and SHK were. He replied:

"Well, the latest thing was *Sewer Cunt* from '94. We started working on issue No 2, but then he got sick. I'm interviewed on the *No Sense* video, on Manson. He did 7" covers for a Manson tribute tape I put out (*Watching Satan*, great colour cover; his 'band' Anus Presley also has a track on it) and the earlier compilation *Magnetic Monster*. I wrote in zines he made earlier, like *Voodoo Epileptikere* and *Skummende Epileptikere*. He did some good-looking layout in a Norwegian zine I wrote for called *Videogore*.

"He did a lot of great artwork for me. Whatever I needed, he always came up with drawings beyond my expectations. I tried to distribute as much of his stuff as I could. I always thought he never got the recognition he deserved. Now, with *Bad Pills* coming out, that will probably change some. But it's too little and too late…

"Apart from the above, we stayed in close touch since the mid-Eighties, exchanging letters, tapes, videos, books, photocopies and records.

SHK, Summer 1997.
Photo courtesy the Kristensen family

Something was always going back and forth, at least on a monthly basis. So you can imagine that he will be missed as a friend and inspirator.

"Last year he did a great drawing for my 30th birthday, and I had a T-shirt made of it."

Team of reviewers
Mikita Brottman
Michael Carlson
John Carter
Simon Collins
David Greenall
Mike Noon
Pan Pantziarka
Rik Rawling
Jack Sargeant
Sarah Turner
Simon Whitechapel
Joe Scott Wilson

All reviews not credited are by
David Kerekes

Send your valuables to

Headpress, 40 Rossall Avenue,
Radcliffe, Manchester,
M26 1JD, Great Britain

ZINES

DERRIERE No 39

£3.99 Gold Star Publications Ltd, PO Box 2028, Whyteleafe, Surrey, CR3 OZQ

Seems like every product these days is the 'New' version — 'New, Fresher' or 'New, Whiter' — and porn is no exception. Always adaptable and aware of the need to 'keep up' with public tastes, porn is often a more reliable indicator of cultural trends than many a survey.

Which brings us to Derriere — or rather 'New' Derriere and, for once, the change is noticeable. I've monitored the progress of this magazine on and off over the years and for all those put off by the consistent appearance of sub-Razzle swamp donkeys, I'm happy to report that all that has changed. A quick flick through this issue is enough to make the heart sing and the juices flow. These girls are all lookers and more than willing to go down on all fours and pull their arse cheeks apart so we the Readers can get a gynaecological close-up view of their rectums. Because, in case the title is too subtle (and judging by the content perhaps 'Count My Rings' would be more appropriate) Derriere is designed specifically for the growing army of anal maniacs out there. Quite what has made anal sex so popular — it was taboo subject matter until very recently in Britain — is open to many theories, none of which are relevant here. What does seem apparent is that despite the cover price being a full £1.50 higher than the ubiquitous Paul Raymond titles, Derriere is a big seller, with new copies flying out the door of the newsagent that I frequent.

With a gloss card cover and top notch paper throughout, Derriere doesn't shirk on the production values, and the photo scenarios don't seem as stilted as those featured in the likes of Men Only. There's little in the way of Readers Letters but what there is gets right down to the butt-slammin' action. Invariably these are two-guys/one-girl orientated, with the first guy permanently wedged in the eager lady's mouth, while the other stud drills away at her arse. The pop shot is always delivered over her 'gaping hole', but doing little to quench her seemingly insatiable thirst for semen... These stories are absolutely pared to the bone; Olympic fit with not a trace of fat, serving only to get the reader's blood racing before he (or she) embarks on his (or her) journey through the photo spreads. For me this issue peaks early with the first guy/girl sequence ('Indecent Proposal') in which a really attractive and stacked brunette with a wide, firm rear, has donned stockings and PVC to cavort with some rent-a-stud (whose head hair is jet black but, curiously, whose pubes are blonde — an intriguing inversion of the usual Collar & Cuffs mismatch). As you'd expect in magazines of this price range, there are no insertion shots (which, to be honest, would destroy a lot of the fantasy aspect for many readers), but our boy's bacon torpedo is at full stretch and often seen poised precariously at the gates of her pussy/arse.

Further in (the mag, that is) we get 'Virgin Fresh' where a girl I recognise from many a Mensworld shoot is sporting glasses, pigtails and posing arse in the air in what looks like a young girl's bedroom, complete with teddy bears and fluffy white rug. She's got a great body but the paedophilic aspect leaves me cold. The two-girl session ('Bottom Dwellers') is a must for blonde fans everywhere but not pubic hair fans, as both ladies sport the dreaded 'racing stripe'.

As is so often the case, the last quarter of Derriere is taken up with ads for phone sex, videos, sex toys and other Gold Star publications. It's interesting to note that the photos that accompany the phone line ads here don't feature any of the inept censorship of the Paul Raymond mags, where mention of anal sex is still avoided.

But the real connoisseur won't give a fuck about that, he (or she) will have flipped right back to the hot brunette photos — revelling in the knowledge that, yes, this is the New Derriere.

Rik Rawling

SHAG STAMP No 5
Jane S. Stamp
£1.50 / $3.00 40pp. Jane S. Stamp, PO Box 47, Bradford, BD8 7TX

Jane S. Stamp is a feminist performance artist from Bradford. She's into Punk and Hardcore and she's recently been to America. She writes about it in this zine. She also writes about being a sex-worker in Germany. If none of that puts you off, the writing shouldn't either: Jane can string a reasonably literate sentence together. I was put off by some of that, though, so the only bits I liked were the old line drawings of Zeus's mortal loves — Ganymede, Leda, Danaë, Europa, et al — and the article that, amongst other things, reveals why having sex with a 13-year-old is an unspeakably evil crime in the UK but not in, say, Spain. It's all to do with a crusading journalist called WT Stead and his exposure of the 'traffic in girls' in Victorian London. The upshot was the heterosexual age of consent being raised from 13 to 16 and homosexual sex being illegal until 1967. Moral: give the powers-that-be an inch and they'll take a fucking mile.

NB. If you write to this zine, don't put 'shag' on the envelope or Jane will get in trouble with the Post Office.
Simon Whitechapel

HELTER SKELTER
No 12 & No 13
ed. Kevin Hogerheide
Write for details: Helter Skelter ent., Westerzicht 94, 4385 AN Vlissingen, Holland

This thin zine offers comic strips and cartoons of varying quality, from the fascinating to the infantile. Mike Diana is the only 'big name' artist amongst the contributors, who are mostly from Europe, mainly Dutch, French, German and Italian. Subjects covered range from the predictable (sex, crime, cannibalism) to the inspired (white trash, Jesus, romance). There's obviously a place and a need for zines like this one, but it might help if the editor was a little more discerning in the quality of some of the material included. **Mikita Brottman**

HEALTER SKELTER
Mondo Xtremo
ed. Alex Papa
£4.50 + £1 p&p. Available through Headpress. See p96.

The fact that Papa has chosen to name his magazine after the words scrawled in blood on the wall of the LaBianca residence in August 1969 — keeping the original misspelling intact — highlights two issues. The first, that this is a magazine with a distinctly Mansonesque

Panels from 'La Vérité' by Thierry Guitard. <u>Helter Skelter No 12</u>

theme to it, and the second, that there are healing aspects to all forms of destruction — the too-often ignored truth of 'regeneration through violence'. This is a zine of superior quality. Glossy pages and dynamic graphics are matched by English/Italian text in flawless translation — a rare virtue in most Eurozines. This 'Mondo Xtremo' issue features a series of intelligent interviews with some of the most interesting and exciting people in the worlds of radical publishing, nihilistic crime, avant-garde film-making and underground art. Manson-themed interviews include face-to-face chats with original Family member Sandra Good and Manson groupies George Stimson and Michael Moynihan. Other interviewees include Jim Goad of **ANSWER Me!**, Norwegian underground guru Jan R. Bruun, John Pirog, editor of **The Necroerotic**, Jörg Buttgereit, cult Mondo directors Angelo and Alfredo Castiglioni, and — to cap it all off — a great article on **Headpress** and an interview with our very own David Kerekes. A truly exciting magazine, professionally and thoughtfully produced.
Mikita Brottman

VIXXXEN No 1
The Fanzine of XXX
Entertainment in Movies,
Videos and Comics
Ed/publisher: unknown. £3.50 (incs p&p) 64pp. Available through: Dark Carnival, 140 Crosby Ave, Scunthorpe, N Lincs, DN15 8NT

There aren't many zines knocking about that set out to cover the so-called 'adult entertainment' industry in all its forms. (Fewer still make it past the first issue.) Well, here comes **Vixxxen**, a zine devoted to doing just that. Presented in

a highly readable and entertaining fashion, no way does **Vixxxen** take itself or its subject matter too seriously. The coverage doesn't become tedious because nothing is dwelt on for too long. No author credits are given, either, and the various contributors — such as The Jazz Master (should be Jizz, surely?!), Jarvis Throat and Rabid Shafter — take great pleasure in sharing their love of the genre with us.

Amongst the many and varied delights on offer are an overview of Michael Ninn's **Sex** in contrast to Greg Dark's **New Wave Hookers 4**; an interview with porn performer Jamie Gillis; and a look at the work of Samantha Fox (not that one) and Ashlyn Gere.

Justin Bomba delivers the two most interesting articles in **Vixxxen** No 1, with his overlook of the world of EROS Comix (with plenty of groovy graphics), and a peek at the odd vision of comic artist Richard Corben. Massive breasts and mighty tools aplenty!

All in all a light-hearted, fun read, recommended to anyone with the slightest interest in the genre.
John Carter

CULTURE GUIDE

THIRD EYE No 5
ed. Mark Coulson
£2.50 48pp. Design House, 17 Brendon Close, Shepshed, Loughborough, Leicestershire, LE12 9BG.

Mark Coulson, editor of this small format, b&w review of 'sex and violence in the media', seems to be suffering from a bout of deep-rooted angst; in the editorial, he laments the fact that the current issue is almost a year late, adding that the New Year makes him feel 'it might be time for a change… or even an end', and asks himself whether **Third Eye** 'is worth carrying on'. Not an auspicious editorial for the New Year, which is a shame, because this magazine's got some good stuff in it — notably, a piece by Keith Breese on Renatto Polselli, another by Anthony Wright on sex and violence in arthouse cinema, and an article by Richard King on the inseparability of sex and violence in the contemporary horror film. The 'gore-drenched, sex-filled film reviews' are equally honest and unpretentious. On the down side, however, take a close look at the seemingly incompatible and random fillers (Jayne Mansfield, Tabatha Cash, Ashlyn Gere and Anna Nicole Smith in one brief, arbitrary 'girlie gallery'), and the amateurish spelling mistakes, and you start to understand what Coulson's getting so depressed about. **Mikita Brottman**

HOG No 3
£3.00 40pp. Rik Rawling, 4A Hardy Avenue, Churwell, Morley, Leeds, W. Yorks. LS27 7SJ

Dear oh dear. **Hog** is a comic featuring sex, violence, sexual violence and violent sex in a manner so shameless that to call it 'gratuitous' would be redundant. The perpetrators — Rik Rawling, Jim Boswell, and Chuck U. Farley (yeah, right!) — seem hell-bent on wallowing (like, er, hogs) in the PC flak their smutty rag would certainly attract if it fell into the hands of right-thinking folk, but I ain't gonna give them the satisfaction. I mean, when they describe themselves as 'guilty parties' and put Yorkshire Ripper photofits in place of author photos, what's the point?

Hog contains three stories, 'Dial M for Motherfucker', The Bitch in 'Pump Action' (no, really), and 'Slutfreak'. Rik Rawling draws better than the other two, though all the women who appear (and there are many) are so obviously cribbed from porn mags that it's amazing they can be made to walk and talk, rather than just crawl round on all fours with their tongues lolling out. It's difficult to see any redeeming value anywhere in the whole mucky mess — the interruption of the action in 'Slutfreak' by a pair of critics arguing about the meaning and worth of it all indicates that Rik Rawling is not devoid of a sense of irony, yet it can't deflect completely the very reasonable accusations of misogyny, immaturity etc. that could be levelled at **Hog**.

Listen — you know better than I do whether you're gonna find an endless parade of chicks with big tits and bigger sidearms fucking, sucking and blowing heads off entertaining (you sick puppies), but be warned. Anybody less jaded than a big Chinese jade necklace (e.g. your mum) is liable to find this stuff seriously offensive. **Hog** is reprehensible… but (sorta) fun. **Simon Collins**

BEEF TORPEDO No 9
ed. "Bob"
20 single-side, photocopied pages, US. Address/price: unknown

These are strange days indeed when this little bugger can pop through your letterbox unsolicited, draped in anonymity. Beyond the golden buns of the college jock on the front cover, **Beef Torpedo** is nothing more than a poorly produced advertisement feature/confessional for gay men devoted to mutual masturbation and DIY. With a very brief appreciation of Tom of Finland (including four illustrations from **The Rope**), a full-frontal shot of porn stars Chris Lord and Tom Chase, this is basically a two article zine. And a surprisingly tame one at that. The first article deals with a visit to a Philadelphia jack-off club called Philly Jacks, a venue I gather is a regular haunt of the editor (check out the web site at http://www.critpath.org/jacks), and the second article deals with a visit to a $28 a night gay guest house in Atlantic City.

Editor "Bob" begins with his discovery of Ocean House, a 15-room men only hotel while browsing the classified section of the **Philadelphia Gay News**. Subsequent investigation reveals the hotel management considers clothing 'optional' on the premises, and warns that self gratification in a room with the door open 'may be seen as invitation for anyone else to participate'. As you would expect, "Bob" just can't wait to pay a visit. The funny thing is, his entire stay proves a total disappointment. The place is run down, sandwiched between derelict buildings, the 50-year-old owner wears only boxer shorts and sandals and — tragically — our editor is the one and only guest! So it's DIY by circumstance for the time being, until, that is, he's caught in the act by the owner who gets spattered with sperm ("Bob" certainly isn't choosy).

After a certain amount of digression regarding various pornographic videos, "Bob" makes his exit only to discover a handsome young man has just checked-in. Sod's law! Despite the veritable orgy that never was, I get the feeling that at least some satisfaction was granted and, without a tendency to exaggerate about his sexual exploits, I believe every word.

And just in case you wanted to know a little more about the elusive "Bob", he gives us a simple tracing of his modest erection on page three ('What I lack in length I make up for in thickness'). It must have been tempting to stretch the truth somewhat with this one, after all, who's gonna find out? In an age where size matters, I'm touched by such honesty. **David Greenall**

HERE & NOW No 18
PO Box 109, Leeds LS5 3AA or c/o Transmission Gallery, 28 King St., Glasgow G1 5QP. 3-issue sub £4 UK/£7.50 Europe/£8.50 elsewhere (£10 airmail).

Though it's about as regular as a giant tortoise on a diet of shingle and superglue, **Here & Now** is well worth waiting for issue by issue: I've been entertained and informed and even influenced by it for a long time. I like its politics, even if I don't always agree with (or understand) them. And what are its politics? Well, I think its editors would say "anarchist", but "sceptical" or "iconoclastic" might be a good qualification of that. Anarchism covers a multitude of sins, after all, and part of what's good about H&N is that it questions and where necessary mocks what other anarchists and radicals get up to. If it isn't already mocking psycho-therapy or feminism or managerialism or post-modernist academia, that is.

No 18 also includes some wonderful piss-takes of the "Zero Tolerance" feminist campaign against male violence and oppression ('By the time they reach eighteen… one of them will be a therapist'). The problem is that the language and thinking of people like that are being mocked in a magazine that is often full of the same kind of language, if not the same kind of thinking. It's annoying when an interesting topic like Satanic Ritual Abuse or the hospice movement is turned into a dreary, semi-literate parade of someone's academic credentials. Hegel? Marx? Debord? All present and correct, sah! As a review in this issue puts it — and it says a lot about **H&N** that it's prepared to report attacks on itself — "The pamphlet includes **Here and Now** in this enemy camp as 'academic shit'." The editors could make a start to improve things by banning use of the word "discourse" and re-printing George Orwell's "Politics & the English Language". That aside, I like what they're doing and wish them long-continued success in doing it. They've got a good eye for an interesting "graphic", too.

Simon Whitechapel

BUKOWSKI ZINE No 4
ed. Rikki Hollywood

£2.50 40pp. PO Box 11271, Wood Green, London, N22 4BF

The Bukowski scene really seems to be thriving since the death of the grizzle-faced old lush, who appears to be gaining the status of a sordid guru for a new generation of European neophytes. For new followers of this alcoholic idol, Rikki Hollywood's **Bukowski Zine** offers a wide and interesting selection of cartoons, comic strips, reviews of Bukowski movies, reviews of other Bukowski fanzines and a guide to all the hard-living drunkard's books and poems. Most interesting, perhaps, is the brief analysis of the 'Beat' and 'Meat' writers and the pages devoted to work of other members of the 'Meat School' — Harry Crews, Jack Black, Edward Bunker and Hubert Selby Jr. **Mikita Brottman**

MIDIAN MAILER No 1

First class stamp/IRC: Midian Books, 69 Park Lane, Bonehill, Tamworth, Staffs, B78 3HZ

Midian have been trading in esoteric books and magazines for a good while now. This new catalogue of theirs sees them ringing in a few changes. Second-hand material appears to be out (it's all

new stuff) and the first half of the publication doesn't consist of books for sale at all, but news, reviews and excerpts from forthcoming publications (in this instance, David Conway's **Metal Sushi**). Free for the price of a stamp.

BUKOWSKI ON BUKOWSKI

£2.50 40pp. Airlift Book Company. Available through **Bukowski Zine**, details above

This slim fanzine dedicated to the thoughts and writings of 'America's greatest realist writer and poet' presents a compact selection of 'Bukowski in his own words'. Quotes from the great man are divided into various subjects, from POETRY, HARD TIMES, WRITING, DRINKING and CYNICISM to FAME, SHAKESPEARE and DEATH, and enlivened by Bukowski's own rough cartoons. The quotes are extracted from the Henry Chinaski stories and other of Bukowski's autobiographical and semi-autobiographical works of fiction. As a result, this is really coffee-table Bukowski, Bukowski lite, Bukowski for the dabbler and dilettante, since anyone with a serious interest in the old postman will already be familiar with the works these quotes are taken from.

Mikita Brottman

MAN ENOUGH TO BE A WOMAN
Jayne County, with Rupert Smith

£11.99 186pp, London: Serpent's Tail, 1995.

In 1977, when I was in my last year at school, I — and others of my age — were allowed access during the dinner hour to a new building called the ROSLA. ROSLA stood for Raising Of The School Leaving Age. Allowing pupils to stay indoors unsupervised during dinner hour, was a pretty radical move for the school. I imagine it was someone's idea of preparing us kids for the maturity of the outside world. We had our own canteen, which served a menu different to that which the rest of the school shared. Here I had my first unfulfilling taste of a hamburger. We didn't have to eat at tables either, but could sit in comfy chairs and eat with our plates on our laps. Fortunately there wasn't a TV set, otherwise we'd have been glued to it. But there <u>was</u> a record player.

Kids brought in their favourite albums. It was always the same kids, too, so we

Jayne County, **Man Enough To Be A Woman**.

heard the same records. (I didn't take any of mine in: I didn't want to get any of my Beatles albums scratched, and I didn't think that Bobby Boris Pickett and the Crypt Kicker Five would go down too well.) Punk Rock was filtering into the mass media, and I had a copy of 'Gary Gilmore's Eyes' by the Adverts at home. I would leave the arm of my record player up, so that the single would play over and over again. I didn't just simply listen to the lyrics — I <u>devoured</u> them. Lyrics <u>meant</u> something, and I never tired of pondering over possible interpretations.

Back in the ROSLA, one single that got played a lot — by the same guy who played Iggy Pop's **The Idiot**, no less — was 'Black is Black', a disco record by a group I no longer remember the name of. You'll have probably heard it. It starts off with the softly spoken vocal: 'We like the disco, we like the disco sound/Black is black is black is black.' I disliked disco as much then as I do now, but I found this record intriguing. 'Black is black, I want my baby back/Is grey is grey, since you went away...' What was the significance of the cyclic use of the lyrics? And was the record about someone who'd died?

One day, someone brought in a book about the Punk phenomenon. I remember in it, near the back, was quoted a traditional Polish saying that went something like 'Every man likes the smell of his own farts'. There was also a full-page photograph of The Electric Chairs on stage, with transsexual frontman Wayne County on his knees, holding the mic between his legs like it was a big hard dick. I remember this image particularly vividly, because that day the school priest came in on one of his 'regular' visits, cheerful as always. As he wandered around the ROSLA, speaking to the kids, he picked up the Punk Rock book and flicked through it in his usual detached-from-reality manner. All us kids smirked nervously. I'm sure he saw the picture of Wayne County and the faux phallus, but he just put the book down again, said, "Very good, very good," and mooched off somewhere else.

That little scenario of a Catholic priest maybe seeing this guy on his knees pretending to masturbate is what I think of when I think of Wayne County.

Wayne County was just too ugly to achieve any kind of major Punk success. His band had a record called 'Fuck Off' (which remains the only record of theirs I've ever heard), he dressed like a woman, changed his name to Jayne, had the chop and became a woman. That's got to make for a pretty interesting autobiography... Indeed, **Man Enough to be a Woman** is such a colourful story that if it was a work of fiction it'd be toned down for credibility's sake. The Punk Rock years take up only a fraction of the book's page count — I was expecting more. Still, I was pleasantly surprised by County's fairy tale pre-Punk history, associating with the likes of Holly Woodlawn, Andy Warhol, Patti Smith, Debbie Harry, the Kinks... Not forgetting the bum record deals, being harassed by both straights and gays, having an early backing band called the Backstreet Boys, meeting Brian Tilsey out of **Coronation Street**, driving across England in a transit van on tour with the Police as support ("The Police were the most boring people I have ever met," says County), playing the Reading Festival in 1977, going on between Hawkwind and the Doobie Brothers and being bottled off...

I don't know what kind of promotion and distribution this book originally got, but I assume not much; this is the only copy I've seen on sale and I bought it — it was published in 1995, but I picked it up new only a couple of months ago. After finishing reading it, I still had no inclination to hear another Electric Chairs record. And my story about the ROSLA and the priest is more interesting anyway.

HOW TO DRAW & SELL COMIC STRIPS
Alan McKenzie

£9.99 144pp, London: Titan Books, 1998. This is a book on How to Draw Comics for people who've never seen a comic. Which begs the question — if you've never really looked at comics before why

would you suddenly want to draw them? It's like never listening to Rock music but wanting to be in a band. And so from this flawed premise, Alan McKenzie attempts to fashion the definitive guide to that most maligned of mediums. And fails.

A bit of background first: Alan McKenzie used to work in some editorial capacity at **2000AD**, until he left/got ousted in one of their increasingly Premier League-like management reshuffles. He did not work there when the comic was any good. For the first three years or so **2000AD** was great — a mutant mishmash of ideas ripped-off from American movies and the warped imaginations of genuine talents like Pat Mills, Kevin O'Neill and John Wagner. Eventually the bubble burst and the title began its inexorable slide into the sewer of quality that it inhabits at present. McKenzie has no innocent part in the story of its demise — under his captainship it plumbed new depths of banality and crassness, employing on the way some of the shittest artists ever to waste tree pulp. His choice of what to publish was a fair indication of his 'taste' and this is reflected in his choice of examples chosen to illustrate the book. He couldn't hope to do a realistic overview of comics without at least touching on the work of Will Eisner or Moebius, but often sidelines their seminal contributions to the medium in favour of twats like Rob Liefeld which, to me, is like placing a pint of Newcastle Brown next to a jam jar of wino piss.

The majority of **How to Draw & Sell Comics** is taken up with step-by-step tips on how to create from scratch an actual comic strip, with entire chapters devoted to script writing, composition, pencilling and inking, lettering and colouring. Each separate 'discipline' is reasonably well covered with side-bar comments that so consistently state the obvious that I had to wonder if this was some attempt at irony. *'A radio is a useful source of inspiration for artists but it can be distracting for writers.'* He's obviously a fan of the production-line approach to comics which, while certainly ensuring that titles meet deadlines, often leads to a piss-weak diluted quality.

Throughout, there is artwork from Steve Parkhouse — one of the best cartoonists around. His energetic linework kept me turning the pages long after I had given up on the author having anything of interest to say. My main problem with the book is that McKenzie's approach is so anal it

removes all the potential joy to be had from working in the medium. But then, his advice is aimed at the eventual 'journeyman' artists and writers who clog up the comic shop shelves every week offering nothing new whatsoever — in which case, he's probably written a masterpiece. He just seems to have no joy for comics, there's not one trace of enthusiasm in any of this book's 144 pages, and producing what is the equivalent of a Department of Transport Major Roadworks pamphlet is not going to bring to the medium any of the fresh and exciting creators that it desperately needs. Fortunately, these wild-eyed crazy innovators will continue to learn their craft their own way and bring us visions far removed from the tedious mainstream that Alan McKenzie is so fond of. **Rik Rawling**

PREACHER
Ancient History
Garth Ennis, Steve Pugh, Richard Case, Carlos Ezquerra

£9.99 222pp, London: Titan Books, 1998. With the mainstream comics industry 'declining' (to be polite) or 'on its knees' (to be more accurate), I suppose it's easy to stand out from the dross. Above all the pointless Soaperheroics and tired, tired fucking tired posturing of Judge Dredd and Batman and all the rest, the only title worthy of any attention is Garth Ennis and Steve Dillons' **Preacher**. Published under DC's Vertigo imprint it caused a seismic upheaval when it first appeared. The creators seemed to revel in a new found sense of freedom — the release of certain editorial constraints allowing them to deal in more graphic depictions of 'adult' themes and to throw in plenty of "Motherfuckers" and "Cocksuckers" to hammer the point home. Those first few issues were exciting to read, simply because, beyond the rabid appropriation

Background Readers draw comics.

of cinematic styles and motifs, it was obvious the guys were having a whale of a time and that enthusiasm pulsed through every line, every panel. Of course, the punishing monthly deadlines have sapped their energies somewhat, but for sheer attitude it is certainly the only 'punk' product published by the big companies and the only one guaranteed to freak out your parents if they caught you reading it. Primarily concerned with a lapsed priest 'possessed' by a 'spirit' that is the offspring of a Demon and Angel copulation (no, honestly), its main theme seems to be an attempt to lay the responsibility for a fucked up world on an AWOL God, using Diseased America as the backdrop. Seemingly unwieldy on paper, it is clear Ennis knows his destination and he's going to try and shock and entertain us along the way. Of course, it's the supporting characters that make this venture all the more interesting. He's far too precious with his main characters, far too respectful of the myths he's paying homage to, but when he lets rip with his more 'disposable' creations it means, usually, more meat for the balcony.

Sadly not so with this collection of **Preacher** specials — strips related to but not necessarily featuring any of the lead characters. First up is 'Saint of Killers' where a Civil War veteran is so shit upon by life that he ends up in Hell, and so full of hate that the Eternal Lake of Fire freezes over — much to the consternation of a foul-mouthed, cigar sucking Satan. Naturally Old Nick is none too happy about this, so, tired of his work, offers to hand the job over to the man who can only feel hate. The Saint of Killers is born and from then on exists as the manifestation of merciless and relentless destruction.

It <u>should</u> have been real rip-roaring stuff, but Ennis fails to really make the most of its potential. His firmly entrenched views of good and evil, heaven and hell only get in the way. Visually there's plenty of bloody action, but the main artist Steve Pugh just <u>isn't</u> up for the job. Overly reliant on photoreference and employing a way-too-bold clear line style, he kills any pace and mood as you pause to study another crap panel. Only the scenes in Hell, rendered by the Spanish master Carlos Ezquerra, really work as he obviously rises to the challenge of depicting the Underworld.

Next up is 'The Story of You Know Who', You Know Who being the series' comic relief 'Arseface' — a teenager inspired by the shotgun suicide of Kurt

Cobain to do likewise — only to survive and be left hideously disfigured with a face that quite literally looks like an Arse. And that's it. That's all you need to know. Quite why they felt the need to fill the 'gaps' in this easily predictable story is beyond me. Dull, pointless and not even the fake porn mag titles (**Ham Javelin**, **Anal Spittoon**) can save it. Last of the lot is 'The Good 'Ole Boys' featuring Jody & T.C. — ultraviolent hillbilly trash who, in the actual series proper, lived and died as violent scum. Here they're played off very much as anti-heroes of the most extreme kind and it's only in the context of a spoof on crap, shelf-filler action video schlock that they can even function in that role. Sadly the spoof is poorly handled, making the classic mistake of not being <u>funny</u>. Like a Hale & Pace, sketch the potential is wasted by failing to understand the intelligence of the audience. I know this is comics and a lack of subtlety is a prerequisite, but for fuck's sake, <u>think</u> before you write! The author's usual obsessions — deviant sex, violent anal intrusion, feisty women and dipstick men — are slapped down with broad brush strokes and all from a nauseously 'apologetic male' perspective. Only the extremity of the violence, the energy of

Ezquerra's artwork and the skewed profanity of the head villain keeps you trucking on to the end. As absolutely disposable trash it's nowhere near as deranged or as deliberately stupid as it should've been.

This collection will surely only appeal to **Preacher** fans who didn't pick up the original comics. Its ultimate lack of audacity will win over no new readers.
Rik Rawling

SEX, STUPIDITY AND GREED Inside the American Movie Industry
Ian Grey

£11.99 (?) 235pp, NY: Juno Books, 1997.
Here you go, a look at the mainstream Hollywood movie biz by someone who much prefers cheap horror movies. The end result, not surprisingly, doesn't come as a huge tinseltown thumbs-up. Author Ian Grey doesn't set out to systematically attack the movies themselves, or their makers in his book, he takes a hard-line Gonzo approach and goes to Hollywood parties. Sometimes he sits and watches television chat shows. Sometimes he tries to track down the copyright on a lousy movie still so that he might use it as an illustration in his book (the still belongs

to **Heathers**, and several phone calls to several different companies and Grey is still non the wiser). You see, **Sex, Stupidity and Greed** is as much about the absurdity of the nature of the beast — the protocol of movie-making today, the manipulation of the public, having a 14-screen multiplex and showing **Jurassic Park 2** on seven of its screens — as it is about shitty multi-million dollar box-office hits (although they do get a look-in). It investigates the frightening control that a handful of mega-corporations have over the entire media and entertainment industry, and how Blockbuster Video, after a film has already been rated by the MPAA, might enforce further cuts should they feel a title in its present form be unsuitable for rental from their stores. Grey speaks to Hollywood insiders — the ones, that is, who agree to be interviewed for a book that isn't published by a subsidiary of their own company — and comes up with some startling information. For instance, read about Roger Corman's **The Fantastic Four**, and the logistics that lead a studio to finance a film they never intended to release...

One chapter is devoted to the fiasco that started out as Richard Stanley's dream project, **The Island of Dr Moreau** (though Stanley was promptly thrown off the set once shooting had started). Grey claims that the resultant movie — which the studios stopped touting as a horror picture and started to claim was campy good fun — is the only movie to have emerged from Hollywood in years that leaves any lasting impression. Why? Because it's a fuck-up on a monumental scale.

I went out and rented **The Island of Dr Moreau** after reading Grey's revisonary stance on the notorious turkey, and <u>didn't</u> find it fun in a good bad-film way. (Though I did find the casting to be 'peculiar' — Marlon Brando... Val Kilmer... David Thewlis...) Similarly, I don't agree with Grey's dismissal of **Con Air**. If **Dr Moreau** can be said to be bad even by blockhead Hollywood standards, then Hollywood must, by the same token, be capable of getting its own formula right sometimes, and producing cliché-driven, high-octane nuggets... of which **Con Air**, to date, is easily the biggest and the best.

But, like I said earlier, this isn't a book about the movies themselves, it's a book about the <u>system</u>. And Grey would appear to have at least weeded out the problem that lies at the heart of it (it is after all the book's recurring motif and the central topic of more than one chapter). The problem with Hollywood, according to **Sex, Stupidity and Greed**, is breast implants. You heard me right, and I'm not joking: breast implants.

THE TWISTED TIMES OF BELLA BASURA

Bella Basura
£5 (or trade) 68pp, Pixie Inc.
Wordprocessing, 20A The Broadway, Mill Road, Cambridge, CB1 3HA.

A novella (are they still called that these days?) produced in pamphlet form, following the drug- and alcohol-fuelled adventures of the eponymous Bella, who encounters quantities of strange people in various urban settings. Literary references abound — **The Book Of The Law**, **Macbeth**, Blake, Situationism, Burroughs, Lewis Carroll, Kathy Acker and all the other usual suspects — and are quoted with variable accuracy. The writing is energetic and pacey, but somehow it never quite manages to gain momentum in any direction but nowhere, fast. I finished reading **Bella Basura** feeling that it

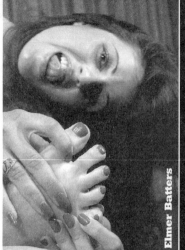

could just as easily have ended 30 pages earlier, or 100 pages later; there is no sense of conclusion or closure, and whilst lots of things happen, none of them seem to have any consequences. The book is not bad, just kind of pointless. To the author I would say: OK, you've done the reading, you've shown you can write, now go and do something with it. **Simon Collins**

GONE IS THE SHAME
A Compendium of Lesbian Erotica
£6.99 598pp, NY: Masquerade.
EVEN OUR FANTASIES
A Compendium of Gay Erotica
£6.99 598pp, NY: Masquerade. Distributed in the UK by Turnaround.

Both of these weighty anthologies (and I refer only to their mass), begin with a learned treatise to assure us that what we're reading has some value. Whilst I've got no objection to people writing intelligently about porn — in fact I wish more people would write intelligently about it — any actual pornographic work that starts off with an essay makes me suspicious. I mean, who are they trying to kid? Come on, let's have some

honesty here... But I digress, both these collections begin with utterly respectable apologia for the pornographic content within.

Once that's over — assured as we are that we're not reading something low down and dirty — we can get to the heart of the matter. Both the books are packed tight with short stories and excerpts from novels, from historical (or pseudo-historical) stuff to newer material of the last few years. Each of the books includes writers well-known in the genre, and these are interleaved with newer names and faces. The male selection includes Larry Townsend, John Preston and Samuel R. Delaney. The female selection includes Laura Antoniou, Alice Joanou and Pat Califia. Interestingly enough, the lesbian book contains a number of stories by women such as Valentina Cilescu and Alizarin Lake, who both write principally for a male audience.

However, given all that, I can't say that these books did very much for me. The Samuel R. Delaney piece was good, but then given the author it's hardly surprising. And the John Preston piece, an excerpt from **Mr Benson**, suffered, like a lot of the material in these

collections, from being pulled out of the context of the novel. Still, if you want a single volume introduction to gay and lesbian porn then these two books are as good as any. **Pan Pantziarka**

THE BOOK OF MR NATURAL Profane Tales of that Old Mystic Madcap
Robert Crumb
£9.99 126pp, Seattle: Fantagraphics, 1996.
Distributed in the UK by Turnaround

Mr Natural is a reluctant guru and mystic who seems to be part genuine and part charlatan. His ways are sometimes so deep as to be impenetrable (he goes to sleep with one shoe on his bed), while his 'enlightenment' often has a familiar ring to it ("Get the right tool for the job"). Mr Natural does appear to possess extraordinary abilities and to be operating from a higher plane of existence, but he also has a very human streak; he has a sense of the theatrical (appearing suddenly in a puff of smoke, going "Ta-da-a-a-a!"), and easily tires of the inane demands made on him by his followers to say something profound. For members of the opposite sex, however, his patience lasts a little

gone generation of smut, with buxom gals lounging around in black silk stockings, panty girdles and slips.

The focus on toes and feet do little for me (other than remind me of the suspect in the Boston Strangler case who got his jollies from watching girls' feet at the cinema — if he saw spread toes, he would ejaculate), so it's something of a relief that LEGS THAT DANCE does indeed paint with a broader, oft times curious, palette. At least one of the women in the book wears nothing but a Pork Pie hat, while another, elsewhere, poses with a pair of industrial shears. One particularly odd shot depicts a lady lying on a kitchen work surface with the top half of her body obscured because it's stuck through a serving hatch...

This is 'cheesecake' erotica. Masses of it. And it comes in a cheesy package, too: instead of the usual plastic shrink-wrapping for protection, LEGS THAT DANCE is sealed by a stocking, tied at the end. A leggy stroke of marketing genius.

ROY STUART
£16.99 160pp h/bk, Köln: Taschen, 1998.

While the models depicted in the Elmer Batters tome [above] are, shall we say, on the chunky motherly side, Roy Stuart's preference swings more to the waif-like. Here we have petite wretches in tiny white pants and blouses, in poses that at times transgress the flimsy divide between softcore and hardcore — I refer specifically to the series of shots showing middle-aged men with their dicks stuck in glory holes, while on the other side of the wall several girlies suck at the disembodied hardened members. Stuart also knows that sexiness doesn't have to equate with stocking tops and high heels: his models have a casual sexiness about them, as if the camera has simply captured an unguarded moment... girls in busy open places 'surreptitiously' flash their knickers whilst crouched down to read a map or take a photograph, or lie in a state of semi-dress on a hotel room bed, half-asleep. (It comes as little surprise that Stuart also offers Glimpse videos for sale — I've never seen one, but I think we all know what they might entail.) Some of the photographs go to create broader scenarios over several pages: like the set entitled Séance, for instance, which would seem to suggest that a spirit enters the body of a beautiful medium in a trance, whereupon the guests strip her naked and engage in somnambulistic sex.

A similar theme is at play in Initiation, where hooded figures have sex with glassy-eyed girls in a dark chamber.

I've looked through this book a dozen times and I still get a kick out of it.

Roy Stuart

longer… (I wonder if Mr Natural has a real life counterpart in one-time Beatles spiritual leader, the Maharishi Mahesh Yogi? For all his pontificating, there is no doubt for a moment that Mr Natural grants his female followers 'special tuition', too.)

Included in this collection are some of the wise one's best adventures. In some of these adventures nothing very much happens (in the strip 'Mr Natural Does the Dishes', Mr Natural does the dishes), while several others entail him trying to set up Flakey Foont — a most unlikely disciple — with a girlfriend. Of course, this wouldn't be Robert Crumb without some contentious material, and here the rub is a series of encounters Flakey and Mr Natural have with the Amazonian 'Devil Girl'. It is what feminists like to call 'objectification' — Mr Natural has the ability to render Devil Girl powerless and do with her body whatever he will; in one strip he 'removes' her head and gives Flakey her body as a present.

CRASH The Limits of Car Safety
Nicholas Faith
£14.99 Boxtree/Channel 4

David Cronenberg's film of JG Ballard's novel **Crash** attracted so much controversy that someone over at Channel 4 must've thought a copycat documentary would be sure to set the cash registers ringing. Of course there would be none of Roseanna Arquette's auto da fake orgasms, it would all be serious and worthy, but there would be plenty of opportunity to air scenes of mayhem and destruction, and audiences would gobble it up. Why else do people watch motor racing?

When Princess Di decided to play Royal Crash Test Dummy, the ante was upped, and how. Of course the programmers would have to observe an appropriately respectful delay, but as soon as they could the programme was out, the promos nudging our Di-consciousness, and of course, the inevitable book of the series followed.

This **Crash** lacks any of JG Ballard's impact. It wants to have its brakes and eat them too. It reminds me of one of those old crime pictures from the Thirties where they spend 90 minutes showing you how cool gangsters are and then tack on some old geezer at the end to tell you that, of course, they really aren't and crime doesn't pay. It could happen to you.

Nicholas Faith deals best with the car industry's long indifference to death, although the sources he quotes, like

Ralph Nader, mostly did it better. He repeats Lewis Mumford's classic description of Detroit's cars being 'a secret collaboration between beauticians and morticians, and based on statistics, both have reason to be satisfied'. Detroit, of course, began to consider passenger safety only after lawsuits turned the cost-benefit tables.

Britain, in its own small way, was even worse. Here, drivers thought of seatbelts as nylon condoms which interfered with the orgasmic pleasure of driving. Alec Issigonis claimed the Mini he designed handled so well that all accidents had to be the driver's fault. Of course the fact that his Mini's front ejector-seats, and easy-off petrol cap made the car a death-trap… well, that was someone else's problem.

The safest cars have always been engineered by those practical, boring Swedes. (Remember when Swedes were considered sexy? It was a long time ago!) In America, Volvo's are cars for college professors. In Britain, they are the weapon of choice for road hogs, or at least they were before women discovered empowerment vehicles, those huge imitation jeeps and Land Rovers which are, according to Faith, the most dangerous cars on the road today. No jokes please.

The movie **Crash** sold itself on the sexuality of mangled flesh and chrome.

So does the auto industry. This book tries to sell itself on sexy car crashes too, but then wants to blame its audience for buying. Shame. And who really thinks cars are sexy anyway? My favourite motor is the mid-Sixties Ford Mustang. Faith calls this 'the greatest penis substitute of all time'. As if!

Michael Carlson

THREEFIFTYSEVEN
Marcus Gray
No 1–20, £4.00 ea, Marcus Gray, c/o John Smith & Son Ltd, 100 Cathedral Street, Glasgow, G4 0RD.

William Burroughs once wrote 'Word begets image and image is virus'. It was an attitude he took to heart and continued to experiment with throughout his literary career. But for all his attempts to 'get past' words, to evolve a new communication medium, Burroughs ultimately failed. What seems strange to me is that the man was a painter as well as a writer and surely during all that time spent out back spray-painting doors and boards (before blasting them with his trusty shotgun), why didn't he realise the truth that had been right before him all the time? A

picture paints a thousand words.

Marcus Gray knows the truth, or at least as much of it as he needs. For the past few years he's been beavering away at his own obsessional work — **ThreeFiftySeven** — and in doing so has furthered the work started by Burroughs (and others) more than any other contemporary writer that I've seen.

Essentially it's a (defiantly!) non-linear 'story', presented with scant regard for conventional chronology, that Gray has self-published in stages via a series of booklets. He's currently working on No 21. Each booklet is hand-made and a work of art in its own right, utilising bursts of plain, unadorned text, juxtaposed with photos, photomontage and images of found ephemera — all colour-photocopied or printed onto acetate. Occasionally there are surprise fold-outs and in one notable instance (No 15) a bag of dice and counters with which to play the board game in the centre pages.

Now, maybe this type of thing has been done before. But I would doubt it's been done so successfully. At last the full potential of Burroughs and Brion Gysin's cut & paste experiments is fully realised, in a work that is sublime and brilliant. The images utilised — sweet wrappers, shop receipts, Polaroids, comic strip panels — all suggest a variety of meanings deeper than the words alone. Sometimes the chosen image relates directly to the text it appears alongside, but, more usually, the relationship is not so clear and often the connection is intended for a line of dialogue or a detail from a previous book… or one still to come.

The story, multi-layered and not easily discerned on first, second or even third readings, is based around Brother Skunk and his relationship with the other characters in the past and present. Multiple viewpoints and flashbacks are used to compound effect — until each scene, each captured moment can be seen through the others — like the multiple faces of a cut jewel reflecting one another. As events unfold, loose ends are tied, only to unfold further down the line.

It's obvious that a major part of this work is autobiographical and barely disguised as anything but.

Gray has tried to have his work recognised by as many people as possible. Letters to Jack Daniels and Levi Strauss for sponsorship, letters to LWT and book publishers have all met with polite and occasionally bemused replies (all of which find their way into the booklets). Ultimately, I feel **ThreeFiftySeven**'s failure to be recognised is due to its very nature: it's not a novel in any typical sense, it's not an 'art book', it's a weird mutant hybrid of several different forms and, I think, unique. Do not hesitate to seek it out.

Rik Rawling

FRANK
Jim Woodring
£9.99 / $19.95 96pp Seattle: Fantagraphics, 1996. Distributed in the UK by Turnaround.

Frank is a cross between Felix the Cat and the cat out of Nard and Pat. He has surreal dialogue-free adventures in a world which, on a good day, is uncomfortably cute. (Frank sits fishing on a lovely green embankment; the sky is blue.) On a bad one, it's a nightmare. (Frank fends off hideous monsters, beating them to a bloody pulp all through the night.) This collection collates several full-colour and several b&w strips. The latter strips are reminiscent of a more European style of comic art, while the colour stuff looks like it wouldn't be out of place in a book written for very young children. I suspect that is Jim Woodring's intention.

On first reading, one assumes that Frank's tales are going somewhere and are saying something. More than that, they must be saying something profound given that they're not at all funny. It is only on closer examination that the reader realises the emperor is indeed butt naked; Frank's tales are not only not funny but they're also quite meaningless. They have a beginning, a middle, but nothing approximating a conclusion. That might seem like a good thing, but in this instance it's simply infuriating. Nice pictures, though.

TRANSIENT WAYS
Jessica Erica Hahn
ELYSIAN FIELDS
Jessica Erica Hahn
$6.00 96pp / $15.00 282pp, Passing Through Publications, 1920 23rd Street, San Francisco, CA 94107, USA.

Both of these books are works of (part-) fiction based on the author's own experience of trainhopping and squatting her way across the USA. They were printed on money obtained through a scam involving state loans, and the venture will "no doubt end by late 98", when this scam is caught onto, claims author/publisher Jessica Hahn.

Both books centre on Una and Malakai. Inspired by Elysian Fields, the Ancient Greek heaven for heroes, these

© Jim Woodring

<u>Frank</u>, the only guest at a party in honour of the dead.

two travellers seek an Earthly equivalent — somewhere to be happy, safe and free. However, the finding of a squat does not seem like a privilege of freedom, but a Hobson's Choice between huge bugs and imminent police raids. It is an idealised freedom, uncomforting and harsh, yet the drugs, theft and squalor throw up an unconventional human morality of their own. Una's ambition is to run a tee-total café, full of cheap food and books. More idealistic (or maybe realistic) than the disturbed and violent Malakai, she turns from him as much for his cavalier response to their dogs, as his aggression towards her.

All the characters live on the pages with insights and personality integral to themselves, not their circumstances. Because of this, the travel, though a central element of the book, loses face to human personality and relationships as a theme. Una is the same person whether traveller or student; unchanged whether seen from a palace or hovel. And the aggressively dispossessed are not improved by any backdrop of place or circumstance. The attitudes, conversation and socio-politico-religious comment of the narrative are more telling of life, and unshattered idealism, than the act of travelling or the travelling person appear to be.

Sarah Turner

JOE GOULD'S SECRET
Joseph Mitchell
£9.99 186pp, Jonathan Cape.

Joe Gould was a little man who hung

around Greenwich Village panhandling. He was a hairy geek in bum's clothes, doing what panhandlers do with a total lack of self-consciousness. Gould was also a Harvard man, from an old family (related, if I'm not mistaken to Robert Gould Shaw, whose fame was recalled in the movie **Glory**). He claimed to understand seagull language, and often tried to talk with them, which was one of the reasons he was known as Professor Seagull.

He was also working on a book, his **Oral History**, and if you paid him or bought him a meal he would read you sections of it. He worked feverishly in notebooks he carried around with him, writing his view of the world and its interaction with his small life. These were reputedly secreted around New York City, and he was well known around the Village. Publishers even showed interest.

Joseph Mitchell wrote two profiles of Gould for **The New Yorker**. The first, in 1942, made Gould something of a friend, and Mitchell indulged Gould a little for about as long as he could take it. Gould's friendship could become obsessive. It was always one-sided, and it also withdrew whenever Mitchell got too close to something he didn't figure out for a long time.

He told Gould's story a second time, again in **The New Yorker**, seven years after Gould's death in 1964. Gould had bummed the streets of the Village from 1916 to 1953, when he was committed to Pilgrim State Hospital on Long Island.

Mitchell's wonderful portrait of Gould

grows from his sensitivity to Gould's own self-understanding. He knew how much of a disappointment he was to his old Boston family. Mitchell quotes two episodes from his sessions with Gould. In one, Gould recounts how he caught his mother looking at him one day when he was young. Tears ran down her cheeks and she murmured "my poor son". Gould never forgot it. Nor did he forget his father taking him to the Boston rail yards to see a new locomotive, when he was 9 or 10, before "he had given up on me", and introducing him to one of the other enthusiasts as "my son". Fifty years later it would still bring tears to Gould's eyes. Mitchell realised not only the crushing effect this pride and disappointment had on Joe, but also the heroic nature of his response. As he says:

He had declined to stay in Norwood and live out his life as Pee Wee Gould, the town fool. If he had to play the fool he would do it on a larger stage, before a friendlier audience.

This is the story of geeks through the ages, though few are as true to their adopted personae as Joe Gould. I wouldn't presume to give away his secret. Mitchell figured it out, and kept it to himself for years before, luckily, sharing it with us in this book. It is a memorial to a place that still exists, even if it comes from a time and milieu that are both long gone. The joke is on the people of style with no understanding. They still live in the Village. And elsewhere. **Michael Carlson**

MAKING MISCHIEF
The Cult Films of
Pete Walker
Steve Chibnall
£12.95 + £1.70p&p. 224pp, FAB Press.
Available through Headpress. See p96.
Another quality cinema publication from FAB Press, **Making Mischief** takes the reader on a film-by-film jaunt through the work of Pete Walker. Most famous for **House of Whipcord**, **Frightmare** and **House of Mortal Sin**, Walker is a veteran of 16 movies (all but one being self-financed) and has a legacy as Britain's most prolific exploitation director. His films are invariably low-budget, but intelligent with it, often providing a deep-seated comment on the social climate of the time. Fortunately, author Steve Chibnall doesn't get bogged down with cinematic and political readings of the films, but offers instead insights that matter — such as the opening credits to

Die Screaming, Marianne being so exciting, that 'what follows is almost bound to be an anti-climax'. Walker also provides a running commentary on his films. He says that he gave the role of sex magazine publisher Miles Fanthorpe in **I Like Birds** to Derek Aylward, because "I thought he was Tony Britton!" **I Like Birds** was also the first 'girlie' feature to receive a general release in Britain, and was padded-out with a 17-minute bondage insert for the benefit of the US market. The insert was a b&w short Walker had made some years earlier for Heritage, who specialised in 8mm 'glamour' and established themselves as a major competitor to George Harrison Marks. Also in the book is a chapter devoted to the unmade Sex Pistols movie **A Star Is Dead** that Walker was set to direct, before the band split and Malcolm McLaren turned to Julien Temple for **The Great Rock'n'Roll Swindle**.

GARBAGE PEOPLE
John Gilmore with Ron Kenner
£10.99 + £1.00p&p. 178pp, Amok Books.
Available through Headpress. See p96.
With this reissue, the big three of Charlie Manson books are available: **Helter Skelter** by LA DA Vince Bugliosi is more about him than Manson, and **The Family** is Ed Sanders' attempt to place Charlie and his dune-buggy attack battalion somewhere off the peace love and tie die map, over where Sgt Fury meets Jimi Hendrix playing Beatle records backwards.

Gilmore's book, originally published in 1971, is an attempt to put Manson more firmly in the tradition of small time hoods who con their way in over their own and everybody else's heads. It's like a Jim Thompson character walking into a psychedelic movie. Because, in effect, when Charlie was released from his wonder years in prison, and out into the just-swinging 1960s, it was like setting a piranha loose in a pool filled with fat stoned sea bass. Guppy power, and all you need is love.

Even more interesting are the Hollywood sleazos who encountered Manson, most of whom had just enough reptile response to keep him at a distance. This included Doris Day's son Terry Melcher, his Beach Boy buddies Charlie made some music, but he also went to Hollywood parties where they looked at him like the ex-con creepo he was. He remembered.

Sanders made much of the family aspect of Manson's family, but Gilmore is sharp enough to realise that for Charlie, families were there to be used, not to provide a source of love. Although there was plenty of the latter about.

Gilmore keeps the story moving better than he did in **Severed**, which was the story of the Black Dahlia killing, and provided an excellent theory for that case, though in hard-to-read fashion. Gilmore's original writing in this book, strangely enough, reads better than the revisions added for this edition.

Bobby Beausoleil, of Ken Anger movie fame, didn't like sharing the credit for his killings. How did Anger ever escape ritual murder, anyway? Beausoleil's gone Aryan Brotherhood in prison, and hates seeing Charlie get all the interviews from today's Hollywood reptiles, the Barbara Walters and Geraldo Riveras of the world. Squeaky Fromme missed

Batman: Four of a Kind.

killing Gerry Ford. Outside prison, the Family lives on. I'm surprised they're not selling souvenirs. The Spahn Ranch will someday be a theme park, just you wait. Helter Skelter City. Every time I see Charlie and his family I think of the local greasers in my childhood neighbourhood, with their DAs and motorcycles, and how fucked up they got when drugs lured them into a mainstream they desperately wanted to avoid. Their chicks were always big-titted and chubby and wouldn't kill anyone if they were told to. **Michael Carlson**

SEARCHING FOR ROBERT JOHNSON
Peter Guralnick
£8.00 82pp Pimlico
They say Robert Johnson sold his soul to the devil, one midnight at a crossroads, and that was why he was able to play the blues the way he did, like no one else.

One night he just showed up at a roadhouse where Son House and Willie Brown were playing, and asked if he could play. Last time they'd seen him he was strumming around. Now he played like a man possessed.

Peter Guralnick wasn't able to track down the devil and ask him for his side of the story, but otherwise, this slim volume is about as comprehensive as we are likely to get on the mysterious life of possibly the most brilliant bluesman ever.

Of course, part of Johnson's appeal is that he died young, poisoned by a jealous husband. The way he played and sang just drew the women, and Robert always wanted one to take care of him, as if he needed protection. Husbands didn't always appreciate this.

But because he died young, there was no success phase, nor decline to his music making. No fat Robert Johnson in spangles with backup singers playing Vegas or appearing on rock and roll hall of fame TV specials.

Guralnick comes to Johnson's music from the days of the fanatic: the Fifties and Sixties, before Clapton and the Stones made versions of 'Crossroads' and 'Love in Vain' popular, before 'Sweet Home Chicago' and 'Walking Blues' were covered by everyone. He has the tone of the true believer, one small step away from the anorak. You really think he'd be happier if the music were only available on 78s, or wax cylinders, still as mysterious as Johnson's life.

Yet he's right about his analysis of what makes Johnson's art so special.

Whatever the devil promised Robert, he delivered. Even though all that is left are a limited number of songs, all primitive recordings, the sheer shuddering power of Johnson's blues reaches through in almost every song.

Voice and guitar seem to meld to produce sounds that rise from some darker part of humanity, somewhere far deeper in the shadows than any of us can imagine. 'Stones in My Passway' 'Terraplane Blues' 'Hell Hound on My Trail' and 'Me and the Devil Blues' have that perfect freedom of art without bounds.

The best part of Guralnick's tale is the way Johnson is something different to everyone who knew him. His contemporaries, Johnny Shines, Son House, Honeyboy Edwards, tell stories that contradict each other, then take on parts of the others' best. Sonny Boy Williamson used to claim Johnson died in his arms.

Even Robert Junior Lockwood, as close to a son as Johnson had, seems at times to be recalling a dream when he talks about the man.

With the advent of CDs, it's easy to assemble Johnson's complete recorded oeuvre. And that raises the one fault with this book. Originally published in 1989, this should have been updated before it was reissued. First, to let us know if Mack McCormick's **Biography of a Phantom** was ever published (I don't think so, but I could be wrong) and more importantly, to update the discography to take account of the CD revolution. But that's a mere quibble.

This is as good a look at the devil as you're likely to get and still retain your own humanity, even have it enhanced. Until Mr Scratch makes his own CD, this one'll do for me. **Michael Carlson**

BATMAN Four of a Kind
Doug Moench, Chuck Dixon, Alan Grant *et al*
£9.99 208pp, London: Titan, 1998.

There are several allusions to Superman being a god in **Supergirl**. This full-page composition in the chapter 'Trust Fund' is one of them. © DC Comics

A collection of tales that, as far as I can determine, interpret four classic Batman stories from way back. Each story focuses on the origins of one of the caped crusader's twisted opponents — Poison Ivy, The Riddler, Scarecrow, Man-Bat — who invariably wind up in Arkham Asylum come the end of the tale. (With the exception of Man-Bat, that is. I couldn't figure why he was here at all. He isn't malicious, nor locked away.)

Of course, each of the deadly rogues starts life as an ordinary Joe, usually picked on at school, then suffering some serious calamity in later life and turning bad. Here they undergo a personality change, adopt a different name, a new identity, and take to wearing outlandish, impractical costumes. (Hey! I'm going to become a scarecrow and go into battle with straw sticking out of my hat!)

Each tale is handled by a different artist and so the style from one story to

CULTURE GUIDE

the next varies considerably. Most of the art is reasonably good — in a mega-corporation, production-line sort of way — but it does get pretty lousy at times, too. Case in point: The Riddler strip appears to have been completed in all of 10 minutes. The intent, I suppose, is 'dynamism' but the actual result borders on the incoherent.

While the whole package has a contemporary look to it, don't expect **Four of a Kind** to be anything more than a good old fashioned superhero punch 'em up. Given the diabolical plot convolutions and cross-referencing evidenced in some of the more popular comics nowadays, that should technically be a good thing, but it isn't.

SUPERGIRL
Peter David, Gary Frank, Cam Smith *et al*
£9.99 223pp, London: Titan, 1998.

Now promoted as a kind of girl-power boss hog, I wonder if Supergirl has managed to recruit many new readers in fans of the Spice Girls? I'd like to think so, but I doubt it — I imagine her readership remains as testicular as it was before.

I've no idea how good or bad this comic book used to be, but I do confess to having enjoyed this 'makeover'. The main thrust of the story is that a group of Satanic individuals are about to

unleash demonic forces and destroy the planet, unless something major comes down and stops them. Into the equation comes an unstable Supergirl, who has psychological problems in that she is now part Linda Danvers, a girl who once fell under the influence of the diabolic group and committed a murder for kicks. The tale concludes as one might expect it to — with a brawl between Supergirl and evil. But there's a lot of interesting stuff leading up to that, with Supergirl turning super-bad (replete with leather pants, leather cape and cut-off 'S' top), half of the city's inhabitants slipping down the evolutionary ladder, organised religion getting a slap in the face, Superman making a brief God-like appearance — all of which is handled with a viciousness and a degree of blood-letting not normally associated with the Super family... Heck, who am I trying to kid? Supergirl — she's a looker all right.

THE SEXUALLY DOMINANT WOMAN
A Workbook for Nervous Beginners
"Lady Green"
£8.99 96pp, Greenery Press, 1994.
Distributed in the UK by Turnaround.

This flimsy, 90-page 'workbook' is devoted to giving advice and instruction to any woman who considers herself

'sexually dominant' — that is, 'who enjoys giving her lover orders, tying him up and/or giving him strong sensations — but part of her enjoyment comes from the knowledge that her partner is enjoying these things, too'. Written by a middle-aged dominatrix and published by herself and her submissive male lover, it's one of those books with little hand-drawn cartoon illustrations and print that runs down the middle of the page only, so you can finish it in about 15 minutes. Still, there are better ways of spending 15 minutes. Most of the advice contained here seems pretty redundant, with tips along the lines of 'check hands and feet often; if they feel cold to your touch, loosen the bondage'. It strikes me that if you're enough into domination to want to buy a book about it, then you probably already know what you're doing. And if not, if you really are a 'nervous beginner', it's difficult to see how your pleasure's going to be greatly enhanced by ticking off little boxes on a checklist, as you remind yourself to do things like 'gently remove the nipple clamps'... **Mikita Brottman**

THE ETHICAL SLUT
A Guide to Infinite Sexual Possibilities
Dossie Easton and Catherine A. Liszt
£11.99 279pp, Greenery Press, 1997.

ART CORNER

PLAY ATTENTION
Marie-Luce Giordani
Photographic Exhibition. Cyberia, Manchester, March–May 1998

In the eco-friendly Nineties we're reminded of the indestructibility of plastic, and worried by its permanence. Marie-Luce Giordani's photographic exhibition, **PLAY ATTENTION**, focusing largely on plastic toys, comments on an alternative and connected permanence — that of the child always submerged within the adult.

Barbie is one of the cornerstones of this collection. This epitome of Californian beach-babe beauty (blonde hair, big chest), and the possessor of a shape only attainable in reality on a seven-foot-tall woman, has been deconstructed — quite literally. Her numerous clones appear wrestling with two-headed plastic monsters, cute snub-nose glass fish or cavorting in various stages of Barbie bondage, decapitation and mutilation. Popped limbs terminate in pink ball joints, while the lava lamp backdrop takes the thirty-something crowd back in time to childhoods where kitsch was pre-retro cool. The exhibition moves away from worshipping the symbols of maturity and success (cars, houses, lifestyles), to an embracing of toys as raw materials. And so observers become little children again, curiously liberated — like Fred, an observer across the table, dressed in fluffy/feathery pink, with gold Cartier footwear and diamante tiara. She is here to view the show, but nestles easily amongst the exhibits.

Marie-Luce is no stranger to effective communication of ideas (she has a background in film, media, language and freelance photography). Expect her next show, **THE BODY** (at Manto in Manchester, Summer 1998), to be as challenging as **PLAY ATTENTION**. Computer manipulated images of the body, sectioned, torn and manipulated, demonstrate the glory of human parts in a shapeless, more approachable abstract. **Sarah Turner**

Marie-Luce Giordani relaxes between exhibitions. Photo © Will Youds

Distributed in the UK by Turnaround.

It's hard to take a book seriously that quotes praise from the pagan goddess 'Morning Glory Zell', and includes an acknowledgement to somebody by the name of 'Joy Wolfwomyn', but then, my suspicions were already aroused when I noticed this book is also published by Greenery Press (see previous review). A closer look, and my suspicions proved well-founded. Co-author "Dossie Easton" turns out to be none other than "Lady Green", author of **The Sexually Dominant Woman**.

This, however, is quite a different kind of book, and not only in that its print almost runs up to each margin. It's a serious look at the values and ethics of what the authors refer to — presumably so as not to be confused with the ageing Californian hippies they at one point confess to being — as 'slutdom'. This is the style of living that used to be known in the Sixties as 'free love', or 'swinging'. In other words, the book gives moral and ethical advice to people of all genders and sexual orientations involved in all kinds of 'open relationships'.

The first part explains the fascinating dynamics of these kinds of relationships; the rest of it seems mostly dedicated to exploring and resolving the jealousies, conflicts, health risks and boundary debates they involve, many of which seem so traumatic and complicated that the authors' children are sure-fire future guests of Jerry Springer. I must admit, by the time I'd got to the end of the book, I wished I was still married. But if you're stuck for a Christmas present for your lesbian partner's co-dependent live-in lover, then this is definitely the book for you. **Mikita Brottman**

SCARY!
Theodore Jouflas
£9.99 96pp, Seattle: Fantagraphics, 1997.
This is the most fascinating, shocking, disturbing book I've come across in a long time. A 96-page adult comic strip, it's described as 'the bastard offspring of "fractured fairytales" and the black-and-white horror movies of the Thirties and Forties'. Deciphering this book is like walking down a grimy funhouse hall of twisted mirrors into the mangled nightmares of some unrepentant psychopath. 'A tale of debauchery, crime, neuroses, greed, lust, psychosis, vengeance, love, rage, mystery, comedy and sorrow', runs the blurb — 'in short, everything about American life at the end of the millennium that we have come to know and savour'. The prose, with its fiendish neologisms, reads like

the work of a lobotomised Lewis Carroll; the print looks like the ugly scrawlings of a serial killer. Imagine Picasso dropping acid with Dr Seuss, and you still don't come close to the contorted atrocities of the illustrations. Imagine Lucien Freud and Edward Lear co-hosting a prime-time US talk-show, with all its trailer-park mayhem, and you still fall short of the insane fairy tale of a storyline. With the art of a pathological vivisectionist, Jouflas uses his neurotic, emetic beast fables to pick at the grotesque scabs of American television culture, exposing all the filthy infections beneath.

Traumatic, sinister and deviant, **Scary!** is the bedtime story for the apocalypse. **Mikita Brottman**

LIBER KOTH
Stephen Sennitt
£4.00 40pp, Logos Press, Cheque/PO payable 'John Beal', 170 Doncaster Rd., Mexborough, South Yorkshire S64 0JW.
The big bad behaviourist BF Skinner once put some pigeons in a cage, added an automatic grain-dispenser, and then went away for 12 hours to give pigeons and dispenser chance to get to know each other better. When he came back, he found that the pigeons had all worked out how to make the dispenser dispense. Only they'd worked out different things. Some of them were hopping on one leg, some of them turning circles with one wing raised, some of them stretching their necks high into the air. Whatever they did, though, sooner or later it worked. The dispenser dispensed, so the pigeons kept on doing whatever it was they were doing.

Are you reminded of something? Skinner was. He called the paper he wrote on the experiment 'A Study in the Growth of Superstition'. I think you could easily replace 'Superstition' with 'Religion'. As far as I can see, the most important difference between those pigeons and Christians or Muslims or Jews is that one pigeon didn't try to kill another pigeon for not believing in the same kind of pointless ritual. The most important difference between those pigeons and an occultist like Stephen Sennitt is that his rituals aren't pointless — they do achieve something. But is it anything more than you achieve from a game of chess or singing in the shower? I don't know. Perhaps that's all anyone can hope to achieve, but even if it is I have my doubts about this way of doing it. Take this ouija-board dialogue from **Liber Koth**, for example:

'What is your name?'
OZ.
'Strength?'
YES.
'I wish to speak to ZOMMO.'
OMMOZ.
'I see: OMM-OZ.'
YES.
'Are you ZOMMO/OMMOZ?'
YES.

My first impulse when I read that was to wonder where the OXO had got to. Yes, I'm afraid I laughed at it. But I'm ignorant about the occult, so I don't want to hold any definite views on it one way or the other. I don't read Lovecraft for ideas about how to perform rituals invoking Nyarlathotep or Cthulhu or Yog-Sothoth and I don't agree with what this booklet says about where Lovecraft got his ideas from, but I could be wrong both times. An occultist like Stephen Sennitt isn't a pigeon, but exactly what he is I don't know. I don't trust what he says and I don't distrust what he says. I just think it's interesting and file it away for future reference. You might want to do the same.
Simon Whitechapel

MEAT IS MURDER!
An Illustrated Guide to Cannibal Culture
Mikita Brottman
£14.95 + £1.70p&p. 213pp, Creation Books. Available through Headpress. See p96.

Our shared human fascination with cannibalism is connected to infantile needs and desires arising in the oral-sadistic phase of childhood development, by virtue of which it becomes a powerfully repressed element of the human unconscious.

Mikita Brottman obviously has

something to say here in this mass-market expansion of her own scribed — and outrageously expensive study — **Offensive Films: Towards An Anthropology of Cinema Vomitif** (Greenwood Press, 1997), but where do I begin? For a start, this is not just about cannibalism in the movies, but also deals with social, cultural and historical elements, linking these with the narrative and structure of popular fairy tales and, in turn, the movies.

Brottman doesn't condemn exploitation cinema, in fact she's rather fond of the genre, but far too much space is taken up with synopsis. Unless you have never seen or read about the likes of **Cannibal Holocaust** and **The Texas Chain Saw Massacre**, the urge to skip pages of text is overwhelming. When she finally gets round to the dissection of such titles, the culmination becomes somewhat repetitive — although not entirely uninteresting — with elements originating in fairy tale lore.

With the exception of Manoel de Olieira's **Os Cannibales** (1988) and Liliana Cavali's **I Cannibali** (1970), **Meat Is Murder** looks only at the popular examples of filmic cannibalism, and many worthy titles are all too briefly mentioned: Danny Lee's horrific **Bun Man: The Untold Story** (1991) for example; the same director's **Dr Lamb** (1992) is restricted to a footnote, only to have its 'sickening scenes of depravity' condemned. This is such a shame. If Brottman had focused her energy and enthusiasm at such deeply disturbing and more recent, less well-known examples of the genre, then this could have been a great book.

As for being an 'illustrated guide', however, the reproduction of many stills is appalling, and I do wish Creation would up-date their unoriginal cover designs. And while I'm moaning, there's one more thing: Brottman feels the audience of Mondo films consists 'chiefly of <u>that</u> group of thrill-seeking adolescent male voyeurs that comprises the main audience for the traditional horror film' (my emphasis). Now this may be true, but the tone of the sentence is certainly derogatory. Being female, Brottman is obviously outside of <u>that</u> group, but with words like 'explicit', 'transgressive', 'bodily extremes', 'murder' and 'mutilation' splashed across the back cover and Leatherface on the front, is it not precisely <u>that</u> group of people who will be drawn to buy this book? I don't see this as a case of the author biting the hand that feeds her,

rather a clash of interest/intention between writer and publisher.

Returning to the quote atop, I am fascinated with my own personal interest in cannibalism, but being adopted and deprived of the joys of mammary lactation as a child, I am still no closer to discovering the roots of my fascination, or my own penchant for cannibalism: eating cock and enjoying it!

David Greenall

SISTERS OF SEVERCY

Jean Aveline

£4.99 + £1.00p&p. Nexus. Payable: Nexus Books, Cash Sales Dept., Virgin Publishing, 332 Ladbroke Grove, London, W10 5AH.

Like other forms of genre fiction — no, like all forms of information — erotica suffers from a serious noise problem. Gone are the days when you'd have to work hard to find a source of pornographic writing; these days every bookshop has an erotica section. In fact even my local corner shop regularly stocks between 10-20 porn novels, there on the shelf, lined up and ready for the punters to get their sweaty mits on them. That's part of the problem of course. There's just too much smut out there on the shelves. And looking at those smut-laden shelves, the books all merge into one glossy mass. You want SM? Tons of it. You want gay? Stacks of it. You want bitter and twisted; sweet and straight; bawdy romps? You name it and it's there on the shelves. Unfortunately most of it is utter dross. Clichéd, unadventurous, poorly written and taking up too much shelf space. You see what I mean? Noise.

However, it's with some pleasure that I can point to at least one recent title worth the effort. **Sisters of Severcy**, by the pseudonymous Jean Aveline, is a real find; one of the best books from Nexus in a long while. Featuring an excellent cover by Christophe Mourthe,

Sisters of Severcy

JEAN AVELINE

this is the story of a virgin, who, by the end of the book, remains exactly that — technically. One of the problems with much pornographic writing is that the emphasis is on the sexual acts themselves; characterisation, plot, location and narrative are too often sacrificed to the need to excite.

There are no such problems here. The writing is spare, the descriptions of place are vivid and atmospheric and it creates its own unique environment in which the characters grow and develop.

In many ways the book reminded me of the film, **Forbidden Planet**, itself based on Shakespeare's **The Tempest**. The character Alain takes on the mantle of Prospero, though sadly in this case the logical, incestuous relationship he has with his daughter Isabelle is not taken to its conclusion. Sadly Nexus guidelines forbid father-daughter incest, though the book goes a long way towards it. The book does have some faults: there are two strands to the book, one based on Isabelle and the other based on Charlotte, the wife of Robert (whom Isabelle is in love with), and the stories revolving around Charlotte have a different atmosphere about them, and they do nothing to move the story forward.

That said, **Sisters of Severcy** is recommended to all fans of SM, erotica and good writing in general.

Pan Pantziarka

SISTERS OF SEVERCY

Jean Aveline

Nexus. Details as above.

Well, I've seen nine Nexus titles now and though I can recommend Arabella Knight's **Susie in Servitude** as a good read and Aran Ashe's two sets of **Chronicles** as a weird read, I can't recommend this as any kind of read at all. Not even as an enjoyable bad one. It has its moments — a bit of boot-wanking, some sororal incest, some fun with cactus-spines — and there's the usual Nexus fladge'n'fucking, but it's all pretty dull stuff. And if I was complaining last time about unnecessary ringing-of-changes-on-the-names-of-sexual-organs, well, don't call me easily satisfied, because I'm complaining this time about the exact opposite. The only sexual organ anyone seems to have in this book is a "sex":

The captain did not sleep that night, and even when Charlotte briefly did it was with his sex in her behind or his fingers in her sex.

Eh? **Simon Whitechapel**

SEX, AMERICAN STYLE
An Illustrated Romp Through the Golden Age of Heterosexuality
Jack Boulware

£11.99 + £2.55p&p. 242pp, Feral House. Available through Headpress. See p96.

This book is the coffee-table equivalent of **Boogie Nights**. A hipster-heavy shuffle through Seventies sex in all its brazen glories. Whole chapters are devoted to John Holmes, nudism, sex advice (CLAP. IN MINNESOTA, IT'S NOT APPLAUSE), sex mags, swingers, How-To manuals, wanton TV shows, ordering sex goods by mail (NEW! PATENTED ACCU-JAC®)... are you getting the picture? A wonderful, mesmerising homage to less politically correct times, when every advertisement — no matter what the product — clearly offered throbbing dick or pulsating pussy with every purchase. Stereos, exhaust mufflers, socks — you name it, you got a fuck out of it.

ORIGINAL SIN
The Visionary Art of Joe Coleman
Jim Jarmusch, John Yau, Harold Schechter

£19.99 + £2.55p&p. 180pp, Heck Editions. Available through Headpress. See p96.

Jim Jarmusch describes Joe Coleman as probably 'the last great painter of religious icons'. Harold Schechter analyses Coleman's telephone answering machine message (which utilises dialogue from Edmund Goulding's 1947 movie, **Nightmare Alley**). And John Yau notes that Coleman paints with incredibly tiny brushes, 'as if he were examining each subject under a microscope'. These are the essayists in **Original Sin**. Interesting all, and not too long.

Joe Coleman's paintings are fascinating. Subjects have flesh that

crawls, and parables run around the borders. The paint itself looks like it's contracted a dermatological disease.

What's more, with this book, Coleman provides a key to the images and meanings in many of his works, as well as a guide to his own Odditorium.

FATLINERS
d: Massive Faal Arse

1997, £12.99, 18 cert. Screen Edge, 28/30 The Square, St Annes on Sea, FY8 1RF.

From Smile Orange, the people who brought the world **Hunt for the Yorkshire Grimace**, the most revolting film of all time, comes this convoluted opus. The story concerns a wrestler who — under the command of Old Father Time's nuisance offspring, the Inflatable Child — sets out to alter the course of history in favour of the bad guys. He successfully opens a window in time courtesy of a wrestling move known as 'fatlining', and slips through it, first to Ancient Rome, then to the 25th Century and numerous places in-between. Also on the trip are Ooge Appy Daddy (who looks like Robert Maxwell) and the Masked Sidekik, rival wrestlers, attempting to put right the wrongs and set history back on its original course.

All manner of dodgy nonsense ensues — the team find an arm-wrestling Hitler, are turned into an arcade game, encounter Goth wrestlers (one of the film's best moments) — culminating in a wrestling match in the Garden of Eden, with the scrapping prowess of such luminaries as Young Mr Grace, Dr Octopus, Sir Clive Sinclair, and Freddy Mercury ("fighting AIDS").

Like **Yorkshire Grimace**, **Fatliners** is unique, but, unlike **Yorkshire Grimace**, it isn't particularly funny. It isn't particularly easy to sit through either, with horrible sound and every line of dialogue delivered in a pantomime style. It is, however, clever and complex on a scale that makes a mockery of its minuscule budget. My overall impression after the final credits had rolled was that I had just witnessed the **1941** of independent filmmaking. **Fatliners** suffers from too much spectacle, causing near-fatal mind collapse in the viewer.

Smile Orange are marching proudly out of step to the rest of the no-budget film 'industry'. **Yorkshire Grimace** was their peg-leg; **Fatliners** is their other one.

Note Smile Orange are looking for cast and crew for their next project, **The Pike**, shooting mid- to late- August 98. Acting may require some nudity. Physical disability no problem. Send photo and info to: Smile Orange Motion Pictures, 29 Villa Road, Bingley, West Yorkshire, BD16 4EU.

MYSTERIES OF THE UNEXPLAINED
Sacred Places and Mystic Spirits (PG cert)
Powers of the Paranormal (12 cert)
Strange Beings and UFOs (U cert)

Three hour-long videos, £34.99. Reader's Digest Mail Order: 0800 115555

The biggest mystery of the unexplained is why anyone at **Reader's Digest** thought that these videos would be of interest to **Headpress**. I've actually had some experience of the 'Digest. Once, on holiday, I came across a vast stack of copies from the late-Sixties and early-Seventies, full of lurid tales about the hippie menace and the perils of psychedelics, which made for pretty entertaining reading. I also remember in the early-Eighties seeing a **Reader's Digest** article on 'video nasties' which only served to fuel my imagination with more depraved images than I've ever actually come across on screen (although **Aftermath** comes close)... Anyway, what's a condensed book? Is it different from an abridged book? It's another **Reader's Digest** mystery of the unexplained.

As to the videos themselves: they all follow the same format, featuring a series of tenuously linked skits set around one exclusive investigation, respectively a study of a room in a haunted house, the use of psychics in a missing child case and a search for bigfoot. As with most videos like this, the provenance of the footage used is uncertain; real documentary footage is mixed in with feature film footage and **Reader's Digest** reconstructions, with no clear indication as to what's what. Some of it's pretty cool — the STRANGE BEINGS tape has footage of Komodo Dragons tearing some large animal limb from limb, original bigfoot footage and giant squids in abundance. Most of it, however, is dull and often laughable. Ever since seeing **Brass Eye**, I find it difficult to take most documentaries seriously, and the ludicrous conclusions offered up here had me in stitches. An example of the jarringly portentous narration: "They sent in a priest, they sent in a medium — and eventually they sent in the **Daily Mail**."

The occasionally interesting parts have believers and sceptics expressing thinly veiled hostility and contempt for each other, some good voodoo footage and a focus on Tibetan yogis' control of their bodies.

There's very little on why some people have such a strong need for the 'unexplained', which is surely one of the key issues, and the scattershot approach ensures that nobody's going to come away satisfied. And this is really the main problem with this collection. Who are they for? Anyone with an interest in this kind of stuff will, no doubt, already have delved further into the subject. The only possible use I can think of is for lazy teachers to entertain their grizzling pupils for an hour. **James Marriott**

DER TODESKING
d: Jörg Buttgereit
1990, £12.99, 18 cert. Screen Edge: Details as above.

To the disturbing aural fusion of the noises of cattle blended with the sounds of the torture chamber, a naked man unfurls from a foetal position into the stiffness of death. So are we gradually brought into the nightmarish world of **Der Todesking** — Buttgereit's most crafted and thoughtful film to date. A compulsive meditation on the decay of the human body, **Der Todesking** charts the uncanny subterranean connections between a series of unexplained deaths, each occurring on a different day of the week, and a set of letters written on Monday by a stranger, moments before his bathtime suicide.

Disturbingly, each morbid scenario is filmed in a different generic style, so the still-life of Monday's suicide contrasts

dramatically with Tuesday's sudden act of domestic violence; the romantic tone of Wednesday's melancholic confession is heightened by its juxtaposition with the stark post-industrial German landscape that provides the setting for Thursday. And Friday's tone of poignant desperation contrasts strongly with Saturday's pseudo-documentary film-reel footage.

And in between it all, the corpse of the title sequence undergoes its grim journey of decay. Glimpsed in a series of brief scenes separating the longer sequences, its skin cracks and fissures, putrefies and breaks, leaks, oozes, opens up and grows riddled with maggots and lice. Finally, the body blackens and becomes cadaverous; worms crawl in and out of the ribcage; the flesh of the face falls away to reveal the skull beneath the skin.

Without inflection, virtually without commentary, Buttgereit shows us the stark desperation of the human condition and the inevitable decay of our bodily detritus. The film's power is enhanced by its soundtrack of hauntingly offbeat vibrato strings, dizzying camera pans, flickering images and b&w footage contrasted with moments of dark surrealism.

Saturday's segment of documentary-style footage gives us a point-of-view shot of a gunman observing a little girl. An older woman comes and sits down beside her and reads to her a short section from a book. "The runner amok," she reads, "doesn't always choose his target consciously. With his urge for spectacular publicity, he is sometimes trying to correct an imbalance." In filmic terms, **Der Todesking** also seeks to correct an imbalance, countering our ignorance of the daily decay of our own bodies with a graphic testament of dead flesh, in every possible stage of corruption.
Mikita Brottman

SPAWN
Episodes 1 & 2 / 3 & 4 / 5 & 6
£12.99 ea, Medusa Pictures, 18 cert.

A violent animated series based on Todd McFarlane's ever-so popular comic book creation, and which tackles themes of a more adult nature than **Spawn**, the recent live action movie. (Though the recent live action movie does have a more impressive vision of Hell.)

Al Simmons is a CIA agent who is murdered whilst on a mission. He makes a deal with one of the big guys down below and returns to earth. Although

he's on the Hades payroll, Al — now a superhero-suited hell-spawn — undertakes an agenda of his own making: to fight evil. This causes all manner of conflicts, none of which are explored satisfactorily here. Are they addressed in the comic book? Dunno, but they're equally as vague in the live action movie. Conflict means physical combat in the world of popular comics, and Spawn doesn't get to sit and deliberate for too long before some bad guy pops up to fire bullets or throw more hell-spunk his way.

Spawn's sidekick is an obnoxious midget clown (no, that's Mr McFarlane introducing each episode) who steals the limelight whenever he puts in an appearance — not that difficult a task when your lead is a monosyllabic angst-ridden shadowy kind of guy.

Each episode is approximately 20 minutes long, and you get two episodes on a tape. A condensed/cut version of all six episodes is also available as a single 15-rated tape.

DARKNESS
d: Leif Jonker
1995, £12.99, 18 cert. Screen Edge: Details as above.

I have to admit that splatter vids are not really my thang, most of them being both boring and unfrightening and spoilt by special effects which make me laugh out loud rather than cringe in terror. I suppose that connoisseurs will tell me that laughing out loud is what you're supposed to do, stoopid, but who cares? Leif Jonker's **Darkness** is a gore-fest-and-a-half and proud of it.

Small-town America used to be menaced by rebellious guys on motorbikes, but as time's moved on so has the menace. In **Darkness**, the quiet of small town USA is disrupted by the arrival of a vampire who looks like a mean son of a bitch who's been listening to too much thrash metal. In no time at all there's a legion of the buggers, sporting bad hair, ripped jeans and an attitude problem.

The other staple of film horrordom is the group-of-teens-at-risk, and this too makes up the theme of this film. As Anytown is swamped by blood-sucking, body-ripping vampires, it's down to a small group of teens to fight back. Will they make it to dawn?

This is low-budget horror at its best. Of the $6,000 budget, $5,900 went on fake blood and the other hundred bucks went on power-tools (don't mention the **Texas Chain Saw Massacre**!). The gore comes quick and fast, and there are times when I really had to cringe. Cheap or not, the special effects are effective.

If you like splatter you'll love this.

Pan Pantziarka

HOLLOW POINT
d: Sidney J. Furie

1995, Marquee Pictures, 18 cert.

Want to know what the single most striking aspect of **Hollow Point** is? Of the entire cast, John Lithgow gives the most underplayed performance. The second most interesting thing is that, in the packaging, the title of the movie has the letters 'o' and 'i' highlighted. Is that because the letter 'o' looks hollow, and 'i' looks like it has a point on it? Whatever, it proves a distraction from the film itself, an 'action-thriller' which places a beautiful FBI agent (Tia Carrere — she's good isn't she) in a love-hate relationship with a burnt-out ex-DEA agent (Thomas Ian Griffith). Despite their differences, they need one another — and a hitman (Donald Sutherland) — in order to try and thwart a sinister plan to unite Russian, Italian and Chinese mobsters.

There is a completely blasé attitude to gun-play in **Hollow Point**. Much of what I believe constitutes humour in the film focuses upon guns and the use of. There are plenty of ludicrous shoot-outs where one character will chide another with a jolly "Missed me!" every time a bullet is fired. Later on, in a fit of pique, we even see Carrere and Griffith shoot each other in the chest... but it's OK, they're wearing bullet-proof vests.

If you like your action on the brain-vegetable side, where one guy will flee an apartment by smashing through a window despite there being an open door which is closer, then **Hollow Point**

EXTREME FIGHTING 2
d: Frank Belmont (Visual, 1996)
CAGE-FIGHT TOURNAMENT
d: Bas Boon (Visual, 1995)
BRUTAL COMBAT
d: Hitoshi Kaneko (Visual, 1997)

I bet the BBFC just _love_ these tapes — real-life testosterone-in-overdrive tournaments in which two guys get in a ring and beat one another senseless. Bare knuckle blows to the head, knees to the stomach, karate chops to the lower back, whatever it takes to get a submission out of your opponent. Well, that's not strictly true — despite use of fatalistic sounding terminology like 'anything goes', these bouts do have rules, a referee, and a doctor on hand with the power to stop a fight. In **EXTREME FIGHTING 2**, we gather there is no eye gouging allowed, no bollock crushing and no biting. However, one team-mate does shout, "Use your elbows!" in the middle of a fight, and at least one guy to enter the ring looks certifiably insane.

EXTREME FIGHTING 2 (which has a 'special project' credit to **PENTHOUSE** magazine) utilises a round arena, surrounded by wire mesh. The fighters have names like Mad Dog and Pit Bull, engaging in moves called 'guillotine' and 'fishhook'. In **CAGE-FIGHT TOURNAMENT** (CAGE FIGHT 1 on the boxcover), one guy throttles another guy into submission. Again, the fighters are 'fenced' in. Not so **BRUTAL COMBAT**, which uses a standard boxing ring. However, 15 minutes of introductions go by before anything approximating 'action' takes place.

Each of these tapes presents the highlights of a different tournament with all the competency of your best mate's wedding video efforts. We might suffer some patchy dialogue from a commentator — starting mid-sentence, or sounding like it wasn't meant to be on tape at all — or we might have constant references to action replays that never come, but lingering shots of nothingness instead.

The most technically inept of this particular bunch is **CAGE-FIGHT TOURNAMENT**, which comes over like a selection of jumbled-up porno loops with a midi-Rock soundtrack and no sex. It also has some pretty peculiar editing (though I'm sure the BBFC are partly to blame). More than once, in a moment of impending carnage with the fighters "up against the ropes", the shot suddenly cuts to the audience, and returns to find the fighters in a completely different situation. Later we hear that, because of an injury, Rene Rozen will not be fighting in the semi-finals. Cue a still picture of his bloody foot. In an intermission, a girl steps up to help a blindfolded man with his dazzling displays of swordmanship. Her nipples peep out from the top of her bra as she lies across a stool, the sword coming down to chop in half the apples across her neck and belly. **CAGE-FIGHT** manages to be both dull _and_ unpleasant.

BRUTAL COMBAT, however, is a different matter. I suspect that the review copy of this particular gem is not the same as the cut you'll find for sale. It's the only tape here to carry a 15 certificate (the other two are rated 18), but it's by far the most extreme in terms of flesh-pounding abuse. The commentator quotes one fighter as saying he's not in it for the money, but in it for the violence. Another is an "actor... working on the new **BATMAN** movie." And it's comforting to know that the fighter known as 'King of the Streets' is in fact a police officer.

Each fight in **BRUTAL COMBAT** has a 30-minute time limit, but rarely does any match make it beyond two minutes. Just as well, seeing that a fighter might have to face several opponents in the course of a single evening. When 'Red' — who has aspirations to be a Stand-up comic — makes it to the Finals, he has already fought three other guys in the last hour or so, and both his eyes are but blackened slits. His opponent, Fred 'The Mangler' Floyd, has not a mark on him, having won a previous bout by default on account of his opponent not showing up.

"That's a good thing — the safety issue," says the commentator, almost begrudgingly, when a doctor stops the fight to check the cut on Red's forehead.

is the movie for you.

I've seen better set-pieces in a Hanna-Barbera cartoon.

SUSPIRIA
d: Dario Argento

1977, £14.99, Nouveaux Pictures, 18 cert. For those readers who have yet to experience this masterpiece of horror cinema, now is the perfect opportunity, for Nouveaux Pictures have come up with the best print short of a cinema or laserdisc release. Unlike earlier video releases, this Suspiria is both uncut and in widescreen. Seeing the full-picture again after all these years, brings home how harmful and insulting the process of panning & scanning really is: virtually every shot in Suspiria has a symmetry to it; people stand where they do in the shot for a purpose. This influences the way in which the film behaves. Naturally, when the image is shorn for the benefit of a TV screen, this balance is lost.

I believed Suspiria to be incredibly complex when I first saw it (back in the late-Seventies or early-Eighties), and was inspired to come back to it for a second viewing to try and figure what plot twists lay beneath its surface. The story constantly hints at trails which may lead someplace important — the maggots in the attic, for instance, or the strange behaviour of otherwise innocuous characters (Suzie's flatmate says that girls with names beginning with the letter 's' are snakes, then enters a juvenile tongue-pulling contest with another classmate). The curious thing is that eventually, after repeated viewings, you realise that these trails don't lead anyplace at all, and the story is a straight-forward one. Instead, the colours and sounds in Suspiria are the film's subtext.

It is no accident that the dialogue is at times barely audible (after all these years, I still can't make out what some of the characters are saying), while the volume of the music positively blasts from the screen.

Sitting in the (now demolished) Classic cinema, I remember the old X trailer for Suspiria featured still images from the movie, each in a different colour wash, with less harmonious moments from the soundtrack playing over the top. Some geezer at the back of the cinema pondered, not to himself, "What the bloody 'ell is that all about?"

Well, it's about style. It's about the beautification of violent death. This film is so fucking great I can't even bring myself to criticise the slightly muted colours in Nouveaux's print.

DEAD KENNEDYS
The On-Broadway's Last Night Concert
d: Dirk BG Dirksen

1985, £12.99, Exempt, Screen Edge: Details as above. Dirk Dirksen is the guy who ran the DMPO's On Broadway Theatre Nightclub in San Francisco. On Saturday June 16, 1984, after booking live bands and comics every night of the year for 10 years, Dirk was forced to close the doors for good. After more than 3,200 shows — playing host to the likes of the Ramones, the Damned, Devo, the Cramps, Iggy Pop, Whoopi Goldberg — the property interests wanted to try something 'different'. Headlining at the venue on its last night were the Dead Kennedys, recorded here for prosperity by Dirk himself.

The DK's run through many of their hits, including 'Police Truck', 'Nazi Punks Fuck Off', 'California übber Alles', most interspersed with pseudo lounge music over which Jello Biafra can engage in one of his monologues.

"How many of you think this country's a democracy?" asks Jello of his audience at one such musical interlude. "If this country's a democracy," he observes, "how come we got no one to vote for?"

Dirk, who looks a bit like Super Mario, hangs around the edges of the stage as the band plays. When the show's over, he moves in, takes the mic, and advises the crowd that the club is closed and to leave the building quietly. It might be the last night, but there is something about his demeanour that suggests Dirk has been doing this every night for the last decade: hanging around the stage, being seen, waiting for his big moment

on the mic. But then, so what? It's Dirk's club. Or rather, it was.

INVASION FOR FLESH & BLOOD
d: Warren F. Disbrow

1996, £12.99, cert 18. Screen Edge: Deatils as above.

The opening 10 minutes of Invasion for Flesh & Blood harkens back to an earlier movie (A Taste for Flesh & Blood), with fast editing, references to developments we know nothing of, and a stupid-looking alien monster maiming and killing a shit load of different people in a variety of outdoor settings. Still, I wish the movie was as mindless and frenetic as this all the way through — with that monster's huge toothy jaws up close, tearing, and the sound it makes. (No kidding, it goes CHOMP-CHOMP.) Sigh, it isn't so…

The alien monster is still alive and on the loose following a thermal nuclear attempt to destroy it — that much I figured. Everybody in a one-mile radius of the explosion is dead, expect for Sandra, who is actually a robot intent on destroying the alien. She's a 'large-boned' robot, too, who wants to have a scientist furnish her with a more supple shell. That's one of the sub-plots. Another sub-plot concerns two guys out to earn some cash making camcorder smut movies, prowling the night and surreptitiously filming teenage girls getting undressed in their bedrooms. (These segments look like they belong in a whole different picture.) In searching for the alien, Fat Robot Girl acquires unwanted assistance in the form of Foul-mouthed Growing-a-Moustache Boy (whose 'acting' consists of saying "fuck" a lot). Together they wander the woods at night carrying a big gun. Wander is the right word, too — not for a second do these idiots look like they have a reason to be in the woods.

KLAUS BEYER sings The Beatles

Swamp Room Records, 7". Contact: Klaus Beyer Fan Club, c/o Behnke, Bornsdorfer Strasse 5, 12053 Berlin, Germany

Unlike his earlier experiments in sound, with this six-track EP Klaus Beyer doesn't simply impose his own German lyrics over original Beatles records, he has his own Beyer Band playing the tracks for him. First off is 'Do You Want To Know A Secret' (a cryptic Beatles choice, as the Fab Four never officially released it), followed by 'Blackbird', complete with background bird song that muscles its way to the fore, and piano accompaniment by Nora Pirsch, who looks all of 10-years-old. The final track on Side 1 is the highlight of the EP: 'Why Don't We Do It In The Road', a gruff and wayward version recorded live at the Red Saloon in Berlin. Side 2 opens with 'Norwegian Wood', and has a completely wonky mini guitar solo to compliment Beyer's completely wonky vocals. 'Something' loses Klaus in a lavish orchestral score, conducted by Joe Tabu (there's also a picture of Joe on the sleeve, standing next to Klaus who is attired in what appears to be a home-made Sgt Pepper uniform). The final track is another live effort, 'Oh! Darling'. The backing band in this instance consist of top Berlin Rockers, Mutter, and the rum sound quality harkens back to early-Beatles at the Star Club, Hamburg. That should please Klaus no end. [An interview with Klaus Beyer can be found in the Sex Murder Art book, details on page 71.] **Joe Scott Wilson**

DRAGON LADIES
The Grotesque Burlesque Revue/The Macabre Melodrama of Lottie Bone

CD, £12.50 + £2.50p&p. Dragon Ladies, Stanley House, St Chad's Place, London, WC1X 9HH

Batten down the hatches for here is a double-billing of the soundtracks to the Dragon Ladies' most recent performances (see main article this issue). No visual stimulus is required, for these tunes pulse and throb like a milky-cocktail that has been left out in the sun too long. From the not-so-fun merry-go-round of Dolly Blue's 'Waltz' to the smoke-filled xylophone lounge that is Lottie Bone's 'Disco La Krupa', songwriter DA Jones creates a garden of earthly delights with more than a hint of decay around the edges. Cyclic rhythms, punctuated with homages to the Euro-sleaze movie industry of the Seventies — aggressive horns, fractured dialogue, and laconic drum fills — **Grotesque Burlesque/Macabre Melodrama** is a backdrop for a troubled mind. (And it's a limited edition of a 100 only, so you're advised not to think on it for too long.)

SNOW PONY
Easy Way Down

See No Evil, Ltd Edition 7"

The opening riff takes the listener on a dirty water ride down the Thames, with pockets of strange swirling sounds threatening to put a premature stop to it all. But the riff wins through. Boats, journeys, no chorus, and lazy vocals — it all adds up to a flawed classic. The flip side — 'Golden Carriage' — utilises more of the frenetic sound interjections. The only guitar here, however, is courtesy of a distorted noise loop, speeded-up and slowed down. There's a mention of "God", too, and if **Headpress** had a Playlist, this single would be at the top of it this week.

. . . .

Mike Noon's Records

THE DONNAS American Teenage Rock 'n' Roll Machine (Lookout LP). Coming at you like a Runaway Ramones juggernaut, The Donnas are four hot-blooded rock chicks from South City, USA. Not one to expect to hear anything like subtlety, this LP is made for crankin' up real high and pogoing around the house to. If The Donnas were a food they'd be fizzy cola dubble bubble gum. Tasty.

THE INFECTIONS Kill... (Rip Off Records LP). Each time Greg Lowery sheds the skin of a previous band — so far he's dispensed with shambling Seventies punk throwbacks Supercharger and Eighties rock Exocet's The Rip Offs — the sound gets much harder and more desperate, which means his next band is going to sound like Pee Wee Herman in a porno cinema. This is way too aggressive and way too angry for men of their ages — get this and pretend Radiohead and Kula Shaker never happened.

SERVOTRON Entertainment Program For Humans (One Louder LP). Servotron are like, robots, no don't laugh, and they're using rock'n'roll in order to take over the human race. Utilising the basic form of the new wave Devo-style sound may have been a mistake in their programming, mind you.

It's entertaining and catchy for the first few songs but after that just kind of washes over you in a [ERADICATE THE HUMAN VIRUS] muzaky kind of way, like nothing has gone in [PROGRAM RE-PROGRAM EMBRYONIC MODE]. I guess the fleshy ones will have to show them the way for the time being. [JOIN US OR DIE!]

SHIZUO Fuck Step '98 (Digital Hardcore 12"). Digital Hardcore recordings are always good for a laugh, with their supersonic speeds and looter-style sampling, and this one is no exception. With an astounding four billion hardcore beats digitised onto 12" of black wax, each track sounds like a war in the studio. Armageddon Outta Here.

ANDRE WILLIAMS Silky (In The Red LP). Look out Puff Daddy, the original rapper, the originator of the Greasy Chicken, the smuttiest man in Detroit, is back and he's brought his friends from The Gories with him. This collaboration between OAP Williams and garage rockers Mick Collins and Dan Kroha is a mix made in garage rock heaven. Taking the raw, bass-guitarlike skronk of Dan Kroha and Collins's trademark sternum crushing floor-tom drum sound and putting them together with Williams' gravely voice and smutty smutty lyrics — he has an ongoing obsession with the smell of 'pussy' — has resulted in one of the heaviest, freshest garage rock LPs of recent years. If this LP were a food it would be fresh kippers.

PSYCHOTROPEDIA
A guide to Publications on the Periphery

by Russ Kick

£15.95 + £1.55 p&p/576pp/ISBN 1 900486 03 2/Illus.

Available 29 August 98

PSYCHOTROPEDIA is the follow-up to Russ Kick's acclaimed book *Outposts*. A massive survey of publications that exist outside the mainstream, it provides 576 pages of detailed reviews (and ordering information) for a breath-taking cross-section of books, zines, catalogues, and other media.

__Learn about__ the skills no one wants you to have: beating lie detectors, hacking cellular phones, growing magic mushrooms, and giving yourself oral sex. __Get the inside stories__ on the Oklahoma City Bombing, SM, sex work, cockfights, the Men in Black, breast implants, body modification, marijuana, Mother Teresa, Heaven's Gate, offshore money havens, suicide, free energy, juror nullification, bestiality, enemas, secrets of famous magicians, and suppressed treatments for cancer and AIDS. __Discover the work__ of taboo-shattering artists and writers, including Andres Serrano, Richard Kern, Annie Sprinkle, David Hamilton, Joel-Peter Witkin, Negativland, Diamanda Galas, Hakim Bey, Mike Diana, David Britton, and Elissa Wald. __Unearth the scary facts__ about vaccines and fluoride, and learn what it's like to be a real-life vampire.

PSYCHOTROPEDIA covers these and hundreds of other touchy and unorthodox topics. More importantly, it tells you *exactly* how you can find out more for yourself.

What they said about Russ Kick's *Outposts*...

"A sick and twisted, and compelling, example of how wide the First Amendment ranges"
—*San Jose Mercury News*

"Even those familiar with 'underground' literature will find much to surprise" —*Nexus*